AF338256

God's Pattern for Revitalization

God's Pattern for Revitalization

Restoring Order and Purpose to God's Church

Robert Beckett

FOREWORD BY
Scott Sherwood

RESOURCE *Publications* · Eugene, Oregon

GOD'S PATTERN FOR REVITALIZATION
Restoring Order and Purpose to God's Church

Resource Publications
An Imprint of Wipf and Stock Publishers
199 W. 8th Ave., Suite 3
Eugene, OR 97401

www.wipfandstock.com

PAPERBACK ISBN: 978-1-6667-5294-6
HARDCOVER ISBN: 978-1-6667-5295-3
EBOOK ISBN: 978-1-6667-5296-0

03/17/23

To my wife, Joanna, for her constant and steady support in the ministry. She never doubts when Jesus speaks. She is a woman of the Word.

To my dad, Herman Beckett, for his encouragement for doing the work that God has laid out before us. For seeing how he loves to serve the Lord through music and lifting others up through songs about Jesus. For his heart in seeing others come to Jesus. Thank you for setting the example of how to be a true and caring friend to his "buddies."

Contents

Foreword

I find Rev. Rob Beckett's writing to be easy to understand and engaging. Not surprisingly I also find Rob to be easy to understand and engaging. He writes like he speaks, and he speaks like he lives. What you see is what you get. You don't have to wonder what Rob is up to. He'll tell you, and then he'll show you.

In the pages that follow, Rob writes what he lives and breathes: church revitalization. He is in love with the Lord of the church and very simply believes Christ's body should reflect the presence and purpose of Jesus himself. He has led church revitalization effectively, and he has had enough seasons of frustration to understand the plight of those who are ever seeking but never finding. Through it all, Rob has been a follower first and a leader second; he has been a learner first and a teacher second. He does not write as one who is simply riding a pendulum swing away from something. His reflection is measured and borne of the kind of wisdom that only comes from experience.

What makes this book worth the read is its uniqueness in a fairly crowded field.

Teaching on church revitalization often works so hard to emphasize the spiritual necessities and messiness of real revival, that chaos is almost presented as a virtue. Rob emphasizes from the outset that God is a God of order, which informs God's plans for revitalization.

Teaching on church revitalization often features stories of such glorious outliers that regular people in regular places are left feeling impressed but no closer to experiencing it themselves. Rob's lessons are accessible, and I happen to know that Rob himself is accessible. How often do you read a book with the confidence that you could call up the author and he or she will listen to you and invest in you? You have picked up just such a unique book.

Lastly, teaching on church revitalization too often serves to convince small churches that they must become large churches in order to achieve real faithfulness. Rob blows this misconception out of the water and calls the small church not to think like a big church but instead to think (and act) right now like what it is: a community of faithful disciples fully capable of responding obediently to God and receiving God's absolute best for their next steps.

What does that look like? That's what this book is about. Enjoy.

Dr. Scott Sherwood

Introduction

When Solomon had finished praying, fire came down
from heaven and consumed the burnt offering and the
sacrifices; and the glory of the Lord filled the temple.

—2 CHR 7:1

IT HAD TO BE an awesome picture, being present and able to witness firsthand the mighty fire of God coming down igniting and
illuminating everything! As a result, Solomon and all the people of
Israel worshiped and praised God.

Solomon had just finished dedicating the new temple for God
as a dwelling place, and the Lord responded in favor of the new
place. All of 2 Chr 7 is the response of the Lord to Solomon's prayer
that he had prayed in the previous chapter. God confirms that if
Israel obeys, they will be blessed. But consequently if they disobey,
they will be judged. The judgment is meant to bring Israel to repentance, and God assures Solomon that if they will be humble,
pray, and repent, then God will deliver them from judgment.

The king and all the people started this off very well, but God
knew that things would not stay that way for long. So after Solomon dedicated the temple, the Lord appeared to him and gave him
some warnings and reassurances.

Then the Lord appeared to Solomon by night, and said
to him: "I have heard your prayer, and have chosen this

place for Myself as a house of sacrifice. When I shut up heaven and there is no rain, or command the locusts to devour the land, or send pestilence among My people, if My people who are called by My name will humble themselves, and pray and seek My face, and turn from their wicked ways, then I will hear from heaven, and will forgive their sin and heal their land." (2 Chr 7:12–14)

This is significant because it shows that even though the temple was built according to God's specifications and was a place where His presence would dwell, it was not enough. The people still had to obey God and live according to His will. They could not just go through the motions and expect everything to be all right.

The dedication of the temple was a turning point for Israel. It was a time when they could have recommitted themselves to following God and living according to His ways. But as we know, they did not. And eventually, the temple was destroyed because of the people's disobedience.

Even though the people of Israel failed to take advantage of the opportunity to fully follow God, we can learn from their example. We too have a place where God's presence dwells—in our hearts. And like the Israelites, we must be careful not to take that for granted. We must live according to His ways and obey His commands. Otherwise, we will not experience the fullness of His presence in our lives.

This is a large topic, and it is hard to know where to begin. To summarize, there are some primary reasons that we Christians haven't been able to witness effectively in our churches today.

We have let our guard down and become too comfortable. We have become content in our own little Christian bubbles and lost sight of the greater lost world around us. We have stopped being radical disciples and instead have watered down the gospel to make it more palatable to a society that is hostile to Christianity. We have stopped being obedient to God's commands. And finally, we have taken His presence for granted.

If we want to see the fire of God come down and manifest Himself in powerful ways as He did in the days of Solomon, we must first make sure that we are living up to our end of the bargain. We must be obedient and faithful to Him, and we must not take His presence for granted. Only then will He move in a mighty way on our behalf. How far we have strayed from our foundational beliefs! How far we have drifted away from God in our nation's life, in our local communities, and how far our churches have abandoned the power of God's fiery passion in their church activities! We see the plague that Solomon could foresee, the judgments of God.

It's time for God's people to humble themselves and pray, to turn from their sinful ways, because God will hear and respond. God will forgive them. And the land will be healed. That is His vow. It must start with His people, who are called His church. Some will say those promises were for the Israeli people for that day only and not intended for us today. I completely reject that notion because God's Word and promises are eternal, and He cannot deviate from His Word. When God promised that He would respond to His people then, that same promise is true today. God will respond when we are in the place of humbled and repentant hearts toward Him.

God's pattern for revitalization is remembering where you have drifted from. It's turning back to obedience and being radical disciples of Jesus Christ. It's not being content in your little Christian world, but it's going out into your community and being the light of Christ that can change hearts and lives, recognizing that we need to consecrate ourselves over again, humbling ourselves, seeking forgiveness, and pleading with God to bring revival to our nation once again. It's repenting of the waywardness of our relationship with Him, responding in such a way that turns our hearts and affections to God, finally returning to the place that we once occupied as God's people and church. We can do this! We *must* do this! The time is now. Will you answer the call?

This book is targeted for the people of God and churches that are struggling, whether big or small, rural or urban. God is here to remind them that He has a pattern for revitalizing their relationship and allowing them to fully live in His will. May we all learn from the Israelites' mistake, and may we recommit ourselves to following God with all our hearts. This is not a book to beat anyone or church down because of some failure on their part. It is a book to encourage and support the people and the church in that God wants to restore and renew our churches so that they can be places of life for people needing to be born-again. Experiencing salvation in Jesus Christ.

Revitalization is the intentional positioning of ourselves to receive the divine provision of revival.

Chapter 1

A God of Order and Purpose

In the beginning God created the heavens and the earth. The earth was without form, and void; and darkness was on the face of the deep. And the Spirit of God was hovering over the face of the waters. Then God said, "Let there be light"; and there was light.

—Gen 1:1–3

In the beginning . . . If you would take a good look at the world today, it would seem that we are living in chaos all over again. Everything is upside down and sideways from everywhere you look to everything you hear. We see both order and chaos in the first book of the Bible, Genesis. In the beginning, God started with a world that was formless and empty and had no shape. In other words, the earth was in a chaotic state. But God brought order to all these things through His spoken word. God created all things, and through Him all things were made. He brought order to the chaos. That is why apple seeds grow into apple trees and produce apples. Zebras produce baby zebras, which grow up and create more zebras. The earth rotates around the sun, and the moon rotates around the earth. This happens at very predictable and set ways. We set our watches and calendars to the moon's rotational cycle.

Unfortunately, sin entered our world through our first parents in the garden. As a result of this disobedience, the order inherent in God's creation was damaged, and the distortion of this order was infused into everything: confusion took the place of surety, deception instead of truth, hiding instead of openness, thorns and thistles instead of plentiful crops, and pain instead of ease. All the perfection of the garden was lost. Our relationship with God became twisted and distorted, which brought chaos into our lives.

A God of Order

"God's very character involves being a God of order and harmony. Existing eternally as the Trinity, the Lord God is complete, unified, and peaceful. He always acts in a harmonious and orderly manner. He is not chaotic or unstable."[1] The same is true of Jesus and His church. The church is to be the very representation of Jesus on earth, carrying out His perfect will in and through us. The church, God's people, gather in a variety of places and settings—and yet they gather for the same grand purpose, which is to glorify God and to lead lost souls to the Savior. The church is God's idea and God's plan, and no matter what the building looks like or how the programs are organized, the church must be absolutely committed to what God wants His church to be. The church helps to restrain the enemy from taking complete control of everything on earth.

Jesus designed the church from the very beginning for significance and purpose. God created us to make a difference in people's lives. The function of the church is to help to bring people to the kingdom, ones who do not know Jesus, to help them become followers and learners of Christ, to be caretakers of their brothers and sisters in Christ, supplying their needs and strengthening their faith.

What happens when a church needs revitalization? The functions that were intended for the church to operate in fall short of their intended purpose. They now become dysfunctional and ineffective. *Dysfunction* by definition is "not performing normally, as an organ or structure of the body; malfunctioning. Having a

1. Bricker, "Why Is God."

malfunctioning part or element: behaving or acting outside specific norms." Churches needing revitalization have stepped away from the prescribed norms described in the Scriptures as Jesus had instructed them to follow. In one sense of the word, we lose our identity; then we lose our purpose. We must understand who we are before we can follow our intended purpose.

God has always intended for the church to function in such a way that we accomplish His perfect will and care for each other as well. When dysfunction comes, all these aspects fall apart. God has always had an intended rhythm for our lives personally and corporately. That rhythm is to walk with Him intimately.

If you've been around the church very long, you've heard, and I have often used, the phrase *having a personal relationship with Jesus.* This is how we describe our interaction with Jesus. We can find some really great truths in that phrase. We know that we have more than a casual acquaintanceship with Jesus, that's it's a relationship. Like any relationship, it can be deep or shallow. And it always needs to be nurtured. We also find that the relationship is personal. We don't enter it because of our association with a group or because we have a membership card. We come into a relationship because something has happened to us individually, as persons.

However, here's the interesting thing: when the Bible describes how we interact with Jesus, we don't find the term *relationship* anywhere in its pages. The Bible never talks about a "personal relationship with Christ." Instead, when the Bible talks about what we have with Jesus, we find a single word: *walk.*

> *He has shown you, O man, what is good;*
> *And what does the Lord require of you*
> *But to do justly,*
> *To love mercy,*
> *And to walk humbly with your God?* (Mic 6:8)

Several people are described as "walking with God" in the Bible, beginning with Enoch in Gen 5:24: *And Enoch walked with God; and he was not, for God took him.*

Noah is described as *a just man, perfect in his generations. Noah walked with God* (Gen 6:9). Walking with God is not an activity reserved for a select few. God desires all His children to walk with Him. Or consider the book of Ephesians, where Paul uses the word *walk* six times to describe how Christ-followers are supposed to live, to have a relationship with Jesus: "Walk worthy. Walk in love. Walk in good works." God wants us to walk, to live, to move forward in our lives. In Exod 16:4 we read, *Then the Lord said to Moses, "Behold, I will rain bread from heaven for you. And the people shall go out and gather a certain quota every day, that I may test them, whether they will walk in My law or not."*

God has a perfect desire that His people who are called by His name should walk with Him. Whether it is God speaking to the Israelites in the Old Testament or he is speaking to His church today, the intention is the same. When we walk in these parameters, then it is well with our being. Deuteronomy 5:33 describes this promise that God gave: *"You shall walk in all the ways which the Lord your God has commanded you, that you may live and that it may be well with you, and that you may prolong your days in the land which you shall possess."*

What happens when we walk with someone? Imagine that you and a close friend are enjoying an evening walk down the road. What is happening is that you are in close proximity to each other. There is blessedness about walking with someone you care for deeply. A special bond occurs as you walk with another. You talk, laugh, listen, and share your hearts. It is as though you can let your guard down and be free in the conversation or even the beauty of not even being in conversation—but together in the silence. Your attention is focused on this person to the exclusion of almost everything else around you. For just a little while you can reflect on the day and enjoy presence. You notice the beauty around you or an occasional distraction, but only to point it out to your companion. You share it together. You are in harmony, and you both enjoy the peaceful camaraderie. The one you are walking with is the destination and not the place you are going.

The Hebrew word for *walk* used in Gen 5, referring to Enoch, indicates much more than just a journey. It means "Human locomotion without any indication of destination." The picture in the Hebrew is of a person moving forward, one step at a time, but is consumed with the journey itself; the joy is in the walking and not where the person is going.

Walking with God is like that. When we enter into an intimate heart relationship with God through faith in His Son (Heb 10:22), he becomes our heart's greatest desire.

Knowing Him, hearing His voice, sharing our hearts with Him, and seeking to please Him become our all-consuming focus. He becomes everything to us. Meeting with Him is not an activity reserved for Sunday morning. We live every day to fellowship with Him. A. W. Tozer states that the goal of every Christian should be to "live in a state of unbroken worship."[2] This is possible only when we walk with God. No matter where he leads us, regardless of the road, the only thing that matters is that we are with Him.

Just as walking with a close friend requires saying "no" to many other things, so walking with God requires letting go of anything that would be a distraction. Pastor Elaine Briefman, a licensed marriage and family counselor says, "You can say no when you have a stronger yes!"[3] When God is our yes, then all else pales in comparison. If you were on a walk with a friend but you brought a kazoo and played it the whole time, the walk would not be satisfying for either of you. Many people attempt to walk with God, but they bring along kazoo-like habits: sins, worldly entertainments, or unhealthy relationships and it is detrimental to the time together.

They know these things are not God's choice for them, but they pretend everything is fine anyway. The relationship is not satisfying to either of them.

To walk with God means that you and God are in agreement about your life. *Can two walk together, unless they are agreed?* (Amos 3:3). This is a beautiful picture of sanctification. To walk with God

2. Cited in "What Does It Mean," para. 3.

3. Stated during an online class by Fishing4Truth, 2022.

means you have aligned your will with His and seek every day to consider yourself "crucified with Christ" (Gal 2:20). This is where justification comes from—being aligned with. You don't have to be perfect in behavior, as none of us is (Rom 3:10), but your heart's desire is to be pleasing to God, and you are willing to let His Spirit conform you to the image of His Son (Rom 8:29).

God created man for the enjoyment of a walking relationship that involved companionship, dialogue, intimacy, joint decision-making, mutual delight, and shared dominion (Gen 3:8). We were created by God, for God, and in the image of God for relationship—but not just relationship but also a *moving and active* relationship. This was part of the order that God intended for us.

It's not a difficult thing to identify people who walk with God and do so daily. Their lives are a stark contrast to the world around them, like stars in a nighttime sky, they stand out plainly (Phil 2:15). Joy is present in their hearts. The peace they possess is incredibly evident in their lives regardless of their circumstances. They produce the fruit of the Spirit (Gal 5:22–23) rather than the fruit of fleshly desire (Gal 5:19–21).

In Acts 4:13 Peter and John had been arrested for preaching and were brought before the authorities. *Now when they saw the boldness of Peter and John, and perceived that they were uneducated and untrained men, they marveled. And they realized that they had been with Jesus.*

When we walk with God every day, the world cannot help but recognize that in spite of our imperfections and lack of knowledge in some areas—we have been with Jesus.

We are to walk with God. That is the journey of intimacy. It is a journey in which you are so engrossed in the relationship that you become person-oriented rather than destination-oriented because the person is the destination. That's the invitation God is extending to us in Christ: *Walk with me. Walk deeply with me. Let me permeate every part of who you are. And let's go somewhere together. Along the way we'll talk. We'll laugh. We'll cry. But with each step, have faith that I am making you into who I want you to be.*

Churches are to be in the same walking journey with Jesus. He is the head of the church and the one we follow. But distractions can cause us to take our eyes off Him and start to wander about. When a church is plateauing and declining, it is usually because its people have strayed. Chaos is an opportunist. Wherever it can find a crack to get into the church, it will. *Chaos* may seem like a strong word for the condition of a church, but it does not necessarily mean beginning-of-time chaos but rather disorder in God's intended purpose chaos.

On the other hand, *order* implies a neat and logical organization of items, task, or people. When a room is in order, it's tidy and everything is in its own place. As we have already stated, God's universe is an orderly system.

The church is much like living bodies in that they are created in God's orderliness. A human body has a heart that pumps blood through the veins to its organs. The brain sends impulses to different areas of the body to help regulate pain, temperature, respiration, and even thought. The human body operates thousands of other functions for every second of every day. Without these orderly functions, the body could not operate in the way it's intended to. The more that science discovers about our bodies, the universe, and everything else, the more we learn about God's miraculous order.

Just as the human body has certain functions to perform to operate in a healthy lifestyle, the church also has parts of its body that must operate in an orderly way. When the church body does not function correctly, then all parts of the body suffer. Churches in need of revitalization are sick bodies that are out of order, in chaos. If this word seems difficult to associate with a church, then let's use some others in the place of *chaos,* like—

- Disorder

- Disarray

- Disorganization

- Confusion

- Turmoil

- Commotion

- Disruption

I think you begin to understand and relate to the word *chaos* for the state of a church in need of revitalization. You can probably associate some of these words with a church you're familiar with.

What God wants for His church is for it to operate and function in the orderly parameters that he set for us to live in. When we go outside those parameters, then there needs to be a way to bring us back into right relationship with Him and to walk in His ways once again.

A God of Purpose

Every church has an intended purpose for them to operate in that is according to His will. Many use Jer 29:11 for encouraging individuals with the truth that God has great things for their lives, and that's true—but this scripture is intended for the chosen ones of Israel. For our context this could be applied to the church more than to the individual. Jerimiah 29:11–14 reads,

> I know the thoughts that I think toward you, says the Lord, thoughts of peace and not of evil, to give you a future and a hope. Then you will call upon Me and go and pray to Me, and I will listen to you. And you will seek Me and find Me, when you search for Me with all your heart. I will be found by you, says the Lord, and I will bring you back from your captivity; I will gather you from all the nations and from all the places where I have driven you, says the Lord, and I will bring you to the place from which I cause you to be carried away captive.

Those who are called into this purpose of God are those who in Christ tand have been called. Second Tim 1:9 tells us that it is Jesus *who has saved us and called us with a holy calling, not according to our works, but according to His own purpose and grace which was given to us in Christ Jesus before time began.* It was not because of our meritorious works that we are called but rather by God's intended purpose and grace for the world.

We became God's chosen and called through the means of the gospel. By having the gospel preached to "every creature," the call is made available to all: *He said to them, "Go into all the world and preach the gospel to every creature. He who believes and is baptized will be saved; but he who does not believe will be condemned"* (Mark 16:15–16). God's purpose for the church is to carry out this mission to everyone around the world. This is consistent with God's desire that *all men . . . be saved* (1 Tim 2:4). It is consistent with God's offer of His Son as *a ransom for all* (1 Tim 2:6). And this is consistent with the Lord's unwillingness *that any should perish* but *that all should come to repentance* (2 Pet 3:9).

As the church, we recognize that our responsibility in accepting this call that we fulfill our part. This requires much diligence. Otherwise, we will be like the Israelites in the wilderness wandering around. The tragic part of that story is that all were called by God to enter the promised land of rest, but most were unable to enter because of unbelief, which led to lack of diligence!

Much like the churches that let chaos enter, a church that needs revitalization has allowed its purpose to be lost according to its call. We have personal responsibility to remain "preserved in Jesus Christ." Jude uses the same word for *preserved* in Jude 21, meaning "keeping yourselves." This indicates that we must cooperate with God. Peter indicated that we are *kept by the power of God through faith* (1 Pet 1:5). God provides the power to keep us safe, but we must provide the faith to walk in it with Him.

The church and its members who are in Christ are indeed richly blessed: We have been "called" by the gospel of Christ, to which call we responded when we obeyed the conditions of the gospel (faith, repentance, confession, and baptism). We have been "sanctified" or set apart for a holy purpose by God the Father as he works upon us through His Holy Spirit in conjunction with His holy Word. Based on our faith, we are "preserved" in Jesus Christ unto eternal life.

Church leaders please know this: forces of Satan are very much at work. They seek to undermine our faith in Christ. They seek to harden our hearts and to develop an evil heart of unbelief. They seek to make us spiritually lazy and not to maintain the diligence necessary to keep ourselves in the love of God, walking with Him daily.

Churches needing revitalization have allowed some form of chaos and loss of purpose to creep in and diminish the effectiveness of the church body. In the following chapter we will look at the reasons of lost order and purpose in churches that are plateauing and declining.

Chapter 2

When Things Go Wrong

Therefore humble yourselves under the mighty hand of God, that He may exalt you in due time, casting all your care upon Him, for He cares for you. Be sober, be vigilant; because your adversary the devil walks about like a roaring lion, seeking whom he may devour. Resist him, steadfast in the faith, knowing that the same sufferings are experienced by your brotherhood in the world. But may the God of all grace, who called us to His eternal glory by Christ Jesus, after you have suffered a while, perfect, establish, strengthen, and settle you.

—1 Pet 5:6–10

Fifty-six men signed the Declaration of Independence. Their conviction resulted in untold sufferings for themselves and their families. These men knew that freedom that costs nothing accomplishes nothing. Of the fifty-six men, five were captured by the British and tortured before they died. Twelve had their homes ransacked and burned. Two lost their sons in the Revolutionary Army. Another had two sons captured. Nine of the fifty-six fought and died from wounds or hardships of the war.

Carter Braxton of Virginia, a wealthy planter and trader, saw his ships sunk by the British navy. He sold his home and properties to pay his debts and died in poverty.

At the battle of Yorktown the British General Cornwallis took over Thomas Nelson's home for his headquarters. Nelson quietly ordered General George Washington to open fire on his, Nelson's, home. The home was destroyed, and Nelson died bankrupt.

John Hart was driven from his wife's bedside as she was dying. Their thirteen children fled for their lives. His fields and mill were destroyed. For over a year he lived in forests and caves, returning home only to find his wife dead and his children vanished. A few weeks later he died from exhaustion.

Every person who endured such pain, such suffering, and such devotion did it because he not only believed in something strongly but also because he knew that there was a greater cause and purpose.

Every person who has said yes to Jesus Christ and has seen his or her life changed and transformed into something that has a greater purpose is a result of the cross of Calvary and what Jesus did there. Ministry that costs nothing accomplishes nothing. Christians are called to follow Christ, to be holy (1 Pet 1:15–16), and if necessary to suffer wrongfully (1 Pet 1:19). We must go where he goes and share His lot, whether it be on the glorious Mount of Transfiguration or in the sorrowful garden of Gethsemane and Calvary.

The church is called into the same purpose corporately. The church is to be a body of believers who live and serve in holy service. Churches are to be the stations of hope for the world outside and the places of praise and thanks for the believers inside. They are to be the starting points for the mission of God to the world. The church mission starts the moment the believers leave the building and enter the world outside.

First Peter 2:21–25 says,

> For to this you were called, because Christ also suffered for us, leaving us an example, that you should follow His steps: "Who committed no sin, Nor was deceit found in His mouth"; who, when He was reviled, did not revile in return; when He suffered, He did not threaten, but committed Himself to Him who judges righteously; who

Himself bore our sins in His own body on the tree, that we, having died to sins, might live for righteousness—by whose stripes you were healed. For you were like sheep going astray, but have now returned to the Shepherd and Overseer of your souls.

To understand the purpose of our calling we must follow in Christ's steps, as noted in verse 21. This is the call—to walk with God. We know that walking with God requires that we be close to Him. The example for us is the life of Christ. Jesus is the incarnate one, the Son, the visible representation of the Father, the invisible God. For a church to know what God desires for them, they only need to look at the life of Christ. He is the foundational cornerstone and the head of the body. The closer we *walk* with Christ, the easier it is to *follow*.

First John 3:16 tells us that we should live as Jesus did. If we want to be close to God and understand His purpose for our lives, we need only follow in Jesus's steps. The comforting thing about following in His footsteps is that we know he has laid the way for us. He does not ask that we should blaze the trail but simply to follow His footsteps. The idea involves complete identification with our Lord's personal innocence, His patient submission, and His uncomplaining meekness, ready to be the servant and not the one served. We know that as the church we are to be conformed to the image of His Son. The Holy Spirit continues to knock off the rough edges even on our churches. As the church grows, it too matures and is transformed into the image of Christ.

Walking with God is a lifestyle. It's not something we do for an hour on Sunday and then go about our week in another mode. We are to be walking with God every day. One way we do this is by spending time in prayer. Prayer is simply talking to God. It doesn't have to be fancy or flowery. We can come to God just as we are. We can tell Him our joys, our sorrows, our fears, and our hopes. Prayer is a way to stay close to God.

Another way we can walk with God is by reading His Word. The Bible is full of wisdom and guidance for our lives. We see that the purpose of our calling is twofold. First, we are called to be close to God. Second, we are called to follow in Jesus's steps. By doing these things, we will be able to more easily understand God's purpose for our lives.

The path and example that Jesus led for us is found in all of scripture. Jesus did not sin. Jesus hated and abhorred sin. Sin was the result of the fall and he came to correct the wrong that sin caused for humanity. As the church, we are called to point people to the one who defeated death, hell, and the grave. Unfortunately, the church has become too tolerant of sin and the effects of it on our society. Churches must stand against blatant and grievous sin, taking the same attitude toward sin as Jesus does.

When we speak as a church, we need to be as clear and precise as Jesus was when he spoke. Peter writes that no guile was found in His mouth. *Guile* means "deceit or treachery." We must have no other motives other than what the Father would have us to do and say. Jesus said that he spoke only what he heard the Father say to Him.

We know that there are times, as the church in this world, when people will hurl insults and try belittling and minimizing our message. As our example, Jesus did not retaliate with sharp words or comebacks to cut people down. He showed humility and gentleness. How satisfying would it be to get the last word, a sharp retort to insult someone else! But that's not what we are to demonstrate.

When Christ suffered, he threatened no one. It could be too easy to have an attitude of "I'll get even." These are not to be the ways of the church. We are not to stoop to the level of revenge and wrath. God is the only one justified to do such things. Jesus committed Himself to God the Father and His authority.

The purpose of the church is to produce fruit and produce it abundantly. We are to be bearers of the fruits of the Spirit.

Love

Joy

Peace

Long suffering

Gentleness

Goodness

Faithfulness

Meekness

Temperance

Jesus is our example, the shepherd who leads and guides. First Peter 2:25 tells us that you must go through a test before you can have a testimony. The story the church can tell is how God has saved each person in that congregation and that each person has a personal testimony to share with others. The battles fought, the trials endured, and the troubles the person has had to conquer in Christ is a story no one can take away.

When Things Go Wrong

Peter was writing to Christians who were described as sheep going astray from truth, holiness, and happiness. For this reason they were lost, unprotected, and exposed to perils that came to devour them. Their lives lacked a guide, a guardian, and a goal. Consequently, they were straying farther and farther away. Is not this a clear picture of so many congregations today. First Peter walks us through many of the same things that are going on now in our nations churches.

There are many reasons that churches need revitalization and revival. The main issue is that they have quit following as closely as they once did, and they no longer resemble the one they are supposed to be following. They have taken their eyes off the one they had affection for. Their walk is no longer solely about the one they were walking with but about the distractions along the way. They are like sheep going astray (v. 25). Something, somewhere, went wrong along the way. Sheep that are astray drift further and further away from the sight and voice of the shepherd. It becomes harder to receive instruct and direction form the shepherd.

There are many things that can distract a church from its mission. It could be something as small as a change in leadership or something more significant, like doctrinal changes. Often congregations lose sight of their purpose and get caught up in the business of running the church instead of focusing on evangelism and discipleship. This is why it's so important for churches to have regular check-ups and times of self-reflection. If your church is in need of a revitalization, here are some steps you can take:

1. Pray for your church regularly. Ask God to reveal any areas that need attention and to guide you in the process of revitalization.

2. Take a close look at your church's mission and vision. Make sure that they are still relevant and in line with what God wants you to accomplish.

3. Evaluate your programs and ministries. Are they effective? Do they need to be changed or updated in any way?

4. Reach out to your community. Get to know the people who live around your church. See what needs they have and how your church can help meet those needs.

5. Be willing to change. Don't be afraid to make necessary changes in order to better reach your community for Christ.

If you take these steps and pray for God's guidance, your church will be well on its way to being revitalized!

Some may read this and are appalled and offended that I would suggest such things about their churches, but the truth remains regardless of our sensibilities. It does not matter how we may not want to hear it or how we want to turn our heads from seeing it, but the truth remains—something went wrong somewhere. That is how sheep go astray.

I have had a problem with my weight for some time. The problem is not the food I eat, but with choices I make in *what* to eat and *how much* of it to eat. I have been guilty of making bad choices involving consumption of foods like cake, extra cookies, and fast food. The problem does not stop there, however. It also involves the choices I do *not* make—these hurt me also. These includes such choices as not eating enough vegetables, not exercising, and all-around lack of moderation. The truth is that I am overweight, and denying and avoiding the truth will not change that. The scale will read the truth whether I stand on it or not. Until I change my choices, nothing else will change.

I'm carrying over thirty pounds too much weight. My doctor has told me that I need to lose weight and that my health is at risk if I don't. I've been working on losing weight for a while now, but it's been a slow and difficult process. I've had to change the way I eat and make better choices when it comes to food. Additionally, I've had to start exercising more regularly and making sure that I'm getting enough physical activity overall. It's been a hard road, but I'm slowly seeing results. The truth is that I'm still overweight and need to lose more weight—but I'm making progress.

I can lose the weight and get healthy if I make the right choices and stick to my plan. Although it won't be easy, it's certainly possible. I just have to keep reminding myself of the truth and stay focused on my goals.

If your church is in need of revitalization, then the truth is that you made choices along the way that have hurt the health of your church. Peter wrote this letter not only to a persecuted church but also to one that struggled with living out its faith. The difficulty many of us face is not necessarily persecution. Most of our struggles come from a failure to remain constantly under the lordship of Jesus Christ. The secret to an effective Christian life is found in living in His strength, not in our own, in living under His control and not under self-rule. It's easy to serve our Lord when times are good, and it costs us nothing to hold to our faith.

But there are times when we grow weary, when we feel defeated, when it seems that the circumstances of life will surely overwhelm us. It is in moments like these that we choose between dealing with life in our own strength or remaining dependent on the Spirit of God living within us.

When things go wrong in any church body, God has patterns of restoration for them throughout Scripture. An example of revitalization patterns for a church that God uses can be found in 1 Pet 5:6–10:

> Humble yourselves under the mighty hand of God, that
> He may exalt you in due time, casting all your care upon
> Him, for He cares for you. Be sober, be vigilant; because
> your adversary the devil walks about like a roaring lion,
> seeking whom he may devour. Resist him, steadfast in
> the faith, knowing that the same sufferings are experi-
> enced by your brotherhood in the world. But may the
> God of all grace, who called us to His eternal glory by
> Christ Jesus, after you have suffered a while, perfect, es-
> tablish, strengthen, and settle you.

If you find yourself in this situation, take heart. God has a word of encouragement for you. His desire is to use these difficulties to strengthen you, to perfect and establish you, and to demonstrate to you how he wants to care for you.

Merriam-Webster defines *pattern* as "a form or model proposed for imitation; a reliable sample of traits, acts, tendencies, or other observable characteristics of a person, group, or institution." God has patterns for people and churches to be able to respond to their lost direction and purpose. Order is an attribute of God. Even when things go wrong, God has order and patterns for putting things in right alignment. Peter tells us what those tools of right alignment are repentance, prayer, and obedience to the Word.

When we as individuals or churches get off track, there is a way back. We must humble ourselves before God and repent of our ways. This means to turn from the pattern of sin that we have been walking in and to return to God's pattern for our lives. We must also pray. Prayer is talking to God and listening to what he has to say. We cannot expect God to lead us back to His pattern for our lives if we are not willing to listen to Him.

Last, we must be obedient to the Word. The Word of God is our guidebook for life. It shows us the pattern that we are supposed to be following. If we are not willing to follow His pattern, then we will never find our way back to His plan for our lives. God has given us everything we need to find our way back to Him. We just have to be willing to follow His pattern.

Be humble.

Humble yourselves under the mighty hand of God.

—1 Pet 5:6

We are to have a humble opinion of ourselves, with lowliness of mind, not thinking of ourselves more highly than we should. In the case of God, we realize that he is the creator, and we are the created. Being humble for most people suggests a form of weakness. They believe that if someone practices humility, it means he or she is not a "go-getter" and doesn't care about performance or working hard. It's the weak one, they believe, who is humble and is dependent on someone else. Why do you suppose the Bible has so much to say about being humble? Maybe we've got it all wrong—and the one who practices humility is actually the *strong* one.

Humility is an important quality, which makes up *the mind of Christ* (Phil 2:3–5). Jesus had every right, if he had chosen, to exercise His authority and right to rule over everyone. He could have demanded high thrones and wielded power at will. But that's not what he did. He came as a servant, not to be served. He came for humanity's sake and not His own. We too are to have this mind of Christ, not only to preserve peace and unity in our relationships with one another but also to preserve a proper relationship with God. *God resists the proud, but gives grace to the humble*—these words are based upon Prov 3:34 and are quoted by James in Jas 4:6.

A person with a humble spirit is highly esteemed by God (Isa 57:15). Understanding God's high estimation of a humble and contrite spirit, we can see David, Moses, Noah, and Paul as good examples. All these were honored by God to do extraordinary tasks for the Lord. Peter charges us *to humble [ourselves] under the mighty hand of God* (1 Pet 5:6)—that is, to submit to His providential workings in our lives, even if it means enduring persecution, as was the case in Peter's day!

What is the reward for this humble service? God will give grace (show unmerited favor) to the humble. He will exalt the humble in due time. When the time is right, then God will exalt His people who place their faith and trust in Him by humbly submitting to His will and to one another. The Greek verb for *humble* here is in the passive voice, which could be translated, "be humbled." In this case, it is the hand of God that is humbling us. We are being instructed to allow God to humble us. *Humble* here is to submit yourself. It is a verbal description of control, letting Him lead, guide, and direct.

Our dog, Ria, is the perfect example of not letting us lead her, although we have the leash in our hand. A dog that is trained well submits to the leadings of its master. It walks alongside its mater stride to stride because it has understood at some point that it's not in control. The dog may have a leash on, but it is not the guiding instrument of control—its master's wishes are. The master determines the appropriate action and direction.

Ria does not understand any of this. When she knows that we're going on a walk with her, she gets so wound up that she cannot even contain herself. Once we do get a leash on her, it's not to guide her—it's to hold on to her. The leash has a twenty-foot lead on it, and she stretches it to the fullest length. She pulls on the leash so tightly that she ends up choking herself and strangling. The whole episode is embarrassing on our part because it makes us fearful that people are looking at us as though we're bad people mistreating our dog. She's the one doing all the damage—not us. If only she would just understand that it would be a lot easier for her to simply submit. God says to us that if we would simply submit and humble ourselves, things would be a lot easier.

Be dependent.

[Cast] all your care upon Him, because He cares for you.

—1 PET 5:7

Whereas pride makes one self-reliant, humility positions us to recognize and accept our dependence upon God. Pride wants to shine the light on and exalt self, to bring all the attention to *me*. Humility takes the light off of self and back on the one that deserves it. The Greek word translated "care" or "anxiety" here is used to express the burden that comes with anxious care and apprehension. Instead of fighting this, we are to turn it back over to the Lord, because God is sovereign. If we are His, then the only thing that comes into our lives are things he allows. This is where the hand of God is reinforced. In fact, look at what Ps 55:22 says: *Cast your burden on the Lord, and He shall sustain you; He will never allow the righteous to be moved.*

Be alert

> Be sober, be vigilant: because your adversary
> the devil walks about like a roaring lion, seeking
> whom he may devour.
>
> —1 PET 5:8

The verbs translated "sober" and "vigilant" literally mean to be mentally calm and alert, both at the same time. Instead of being anxious, we can be mentally calm because we are depending upon the Lord, and yet because we know we have an enemy, we must be alert to the reality that our enemy wants to use every circumstance of our lives to destroy us. Peter knows this firsthand; he knows about what the devil can do. Jesus told Peter be careful because the devil wanted to sift him like wheat. Here's how the enemy works:

1. **Temptation**—He entices us to act contrary to God's plan and displease Him. Satan wants your soul, but if he can't have it, he'll take your witness. If he cannot have you for eternity, he wants to render you ineffective in the present. Because he knows human nature better than we do. He is an expert at appealing to our fallen nature, our carnal desires.

2. **Deception**—He causes us to believe things about God and ourselves that are not true. He will tell you that you're not good enough, you messed up too many times, or you messed

up so badly that God will not forgive you. Since we always act out of what we believe, we must believe what is true. Scripture says that the devil is the father of all lies and a deceiver. He will appear as an angel of light. He can also take what seems good and twist it. He will get us to do his bidding, making us think we are somehow serving God. We have the Word of God to lead us down the pathway of righteousness, to be a light unto our path and a lamp unto our feet.

3. **Discouragement**—The devil has a way of causing us to question whether or not living for Christ is worth it. The psalmist expresses this: *But as for me, my feet had almost stumbled; My steps had nearly slipped. For I was envious of the boastful, When I saw the prosperity of the wicked* (Ps 73:2–3).[/NL 1–3]

Be tenacious

Resist him, steadfast in the faith.

—1 Pet 5:9

When we have humbled ourselves and found our strength in God, when we have learned the secret of dependence, and when we remain on our guard against the devil, we stand our ground. There is a direct relationship between strong faith and the ability to live an overcoming life. Ephesians 6 tells us to take up the shield of faith and that having put on the whole armor of God, we will be able to stand firm against the schemes of the devil. James 4:7 says, *Submit to God. Resist the devil and he will flee from you.* And here in 1 Pet 5 we are told to resist the devil steadfastly in our faith.

Be prepared

Knowing that the same sufferings are experienced by your brotherhood in the world.

—1 Pet 5:9

Be prepared for the persecution that will come. Paul told Timothy in 2 Tim 3:12, *All who desire to live godly in Christ Jesus will suffer persecution.* As Peter under the inspiration of the Holy Spirit wrote these words to the early church, persecution of Christianity was spreading.

Be assured

> But may the God of all grace . . . perfect, establish, strengthen, and settle you.
>
> —1 PET 5:10

Here we have the promise that as God accomplishes His purpose in us, he will do four things for us:

A. *Perfect us:* Bring us to wholeness, nothing lacking, complete us in every way.

B. *Confirm us:* The idea here is to make us firm. Rather than being uncertain and weak, we will be resolute and determined in our faith.

C. *Strengthen us:* He will use the difficulties to make us stronger, to enable us to face anything he allows to come our way.

D. *Establish us:* The picture the Greek paints for us here is of a foundation that is not shaky but has settled and is firmly founded.

A church that is need of revitalization finds itself so because one or more of the above elements have fallen short. Somewhere the church has lost its humility, reliance, or vigilance for the work in the Lord. More than likely *all* are lacking to some degree.

Getting Back to the Basics

A disturbing trend seen too often in churches needing revitalization is the apparent apathy, unconcern, or "Oh, well" of many

Christians for others and the community-at-large. They may attend services, but it appears that they are only "going through the motions." Their singing, their praying, their Bible Study, their zeal all seem lifeless. To rephrase Henry David Thoreau, "The majority of [Christians] lead lives of quiet desperation."

Certainly, God desires more for His children. Romans 15:13 says, *Now may the God of hope fill you with all joy and peace in believing, that you may abound in hope by the power of the Holy Spirit.* I suspect the problem is one that's close to that of an athlete or a sports team who's "in a slump." Such a person or team "goes through the motions," but they are not performing up to their true potential. The solution in sports: Work on "the fundamentals." The same is true with Christians. When we find ourselves "in a slump," we need to stress the fundamentals. As he addresses the churches from the Isle of Patmos, Jesus says in Rev 2:4–5, *"Nevertheless I have this against you, that you have left your first love. Remember therefore from where you have fallen; repent and do the first works, or else I will come to you quickly and remove your lampstand from its place—unless you repent."* This is part of the pattern of revitalization that God intends for us. We need to get "back to the basics"!

I would like to stress some of the "fundamentals" or "basics" to address whenever things in our lives go wrong:

Energize your faith.

A scriptural definition of *faith* is found in Heb 11:1: *Now faith is the substance of things hoped for, the evidence of things not seen.* Vine's describes faith as "a firm conviction." I like to think of faith as "confident trust." Faith must be of great importance. Faith in God is essential to pleasing Him. Faith in Jesus is essential to finding forgiveness and eternal life. *Without faith it is impossible to please Him, for he who comes to God must believe that He is, and that He is a rewarder or those who diligently seek Him* (Heb 11:6). Therefore, if we wish to have a relationship and walk with God in which he is pleased with us, we *must* have faith in Him. This is non-negotiable.

It is also important to understand that our faith pleases God not because of its perfection but because of its genuineness. God is not looking for us to have faith that is without flaw, but rather he is looking for us to have faith that is real and authentic. So don't be discouraged if your faith isn't perfect. As long as it is genuine, God will be pleased.

Without faith the only alternative is doubt accompanied with fear, fear of not knowing what the future holds and doubting if anything good will ever come our way. When we have faith, we trust that despite the challenges we face, things will eventually work out for His good and perfect will. We may not always understand why things happen the way they do, but we know that there is a reason behind it all. When we have faith, we are able to see the good in people and situations even when it's not immediately apparent. We are more forgiving, because we know that everyone is fighting his or her own battles. We are more compassionate, because we can empathize with the struggles of others. Faith gives us hope that things will get better, even when it feels as if they're falling apart

Faith is what gives us the strength to keep going when we feel that we can't take anymore. It's what helps us get through the tough times and come out stronger on the other side. So don't give up regardless of how difficult things seem. Have faith and believe that everything will work out in the end. Trust that God has a plan for you, and know that whatever happens, it will ultimately be for His glory.

The Word of God is designed to produce faith. When we hear or read the Word, faith is produced in us. It's not just an accumulation of Bible knowledge; it's a life-changing power that comes from hearing and responding to what God has said. As we meditate on scripture, we are transformed by its truth. We become more like Christ—our minds are renewed, our hearts are changed, and our lives begin lining up with God's will.

The Scriptures are living and active, sharper than any two-edged sword (Heb 4:12). They have the power to convict us of sin, to teach us righteousness, and to transform our lives. When we hide God's Word in our hearts, we are better able to resist temptation and make godly choices. We're also better equipped to minister to others, because the Word of God is living and active in us. If you want your faith to grow, start by hiding God's Word in your heart. Meditate on it day and night so that you can apply its truth to your life and see transformation take place.

When you find yourself in a spiritual slump, pick up your Bible and allow it to rebuild that "confident trust" you once had! It will also help you to—

1. Remember who you are in Christ

2. Understand what Christ has done for you

3. Grasp the promises of God

4. Know how to fight spiritual battles

5. Be encouraged by the stories of others

When you read the Bible, not only will your faith be restored, but you'll also be better.

Let your hope be fortified.

When the troubles of this world come crashing down on you, let your hope be fortified by the knowledge that God is with you always. He will never leave you or forsake you. So when despair threatens to overwhelm you, remember that your hope lies in Christ alone. Let His love and peace wash over you, and find strength in knowing that he is always there for you.

A common definition of *hope* is "desire plus expectation." So often our hopes are dashed because we put our trust in things that are beyond our control. But when we place our hope in Jesus Christ, we can be confident that he will never let us down. No matter what storms you face in life, take comfort in knowing that God is with you always. Let His peace and love wash over you, and find strength in the hope that you have in Christ.

Hope is necessary to persevere. It's what gets us through tough times. And when despair threatens to overwhelm you, remember that your hope lies in Christ alone. He will never let you down. Hope is necessary for our motivation to become pure. Hope clears the clouds from our minds and fills us with positivity. Hope is a key that opens the door of opportunity and success.

Without hope we cannot accomplish anything in life. It is like a light in the darkness that guides us toward our goals. Hope keeps us going when everything else fails. It is what makes us believe that tomorrow will be better than today. Hope is what makes us strong when we are weak. It is what gives us courage to face our fears. Hope is what makes us stand up again after we have fallen. It is what gives us the strength to keep going even when we feel like giving up.

Through its revelation of God's dealings with humanity in the past, we know God keeps His promises, so we have hope. The Bible shows us how to avoid making the same mistakes that others have made. The Bible is also a source of comfort when we face our own trials and challenges. Knowing that others have gone through similar experiences can help us to endure our own difficulties.

The Bible is not just a history book or a source of moral lessons; it is also a book that can bring us hope and comfort. Through its revelation of God's dealings with man in the past, we know that God keeps His promises, so we have hope.

When an athlete gets discouraged, he or she is often told, "Keep your eye on the ball!" The Christian must also do this, and it is with the aid of God's Word that we can keep our focus where it ought to be. Philippians 4:8 instructs us, *Finally, brethren, whatever things are true, whatever things are noble, whatever things are just, whatever things are pure, whatever things are lovely, whatever things are of good report, if there is any virtue and if there is anything praiseworthy—meditate on these things.* What a great list! And how often our minds are filled with thoughts that do not fall into any of these categories!

The Christian must learn to meditate on things that are true, noble, just, pure, lovely, and of good report. This is not always easy, but it is possible with the help of God's Word.

Activate your love.

Paul gives the best definition of love in 1 Cor 13:7–8: *[Love] bears all things, believes all things, hopes all things, endures all things. Love never fails.* One of the most beautiful things in this world is love. It is what drives us to be better people and do better things. When we love others, it reassures them that they are important to us and that we care about them. In the same way, expressing our love for God reassures us that we abide in Him and that he abides in us. This is because *God is love* (1 John 4:16).

Jesus is the perfect example of love. He loves us so much that he was willing to die for us. His death shows us the depth of His love for us. When we see how much Jesus loves us, it should motivate us to love others in the same way. We can show our love for others by sacrificing our time, energy, and resources for them. When we do this, we are imitating the love of Jesus.

Enhancing our joy.

Joy is an essential element of what constitutes the kingdom of God. The kingdom of God is not a place but rather a state of being in which God reigns supreme. In this state all of creation is subject to His will, and His purposes are carried out perfectly. Those who enter into this state experience true joy and peace that come from knowing they are living in accordance with God's plan.

True joy is not based on our circumstances but rather on our relationship with God. When we are in right relationship with Him, we can joyfully face any circumstance because we know that he is in control. Our confidence is in Him, not in ourselves or our ability to handle whatever comes our way.

The kingdom of God is a place of perfect love, joy, peace, and righteousness. It is a place where God is glorified and His people live in harmony with Him and with one another. It is a place where all our needs are met, both spiritual and physical.

Enjoy your peace.

A lack of peace often contributes to the "spiritual stagnation" that afflicts many Christians. The following is a list of things you can do that can help you find peace:

- Spend time with God in prayer and meditation.

- Read the Bible and other spiritual books.

- Attend church regularly.

- Get involved in a small group or Sunday school class.

- Serve others through volunteering or mission work.

And having peace with God has a positive effect on our peace with our enemies. Ephesians 4:3 tells us that we should be *endeavoring to keep the unity of the Spirit in the bond of peace.* When we have a close relationship with God, it's easier to stay unified with other believers and to maintain peace with those around us.

But even more importantly, our peace with God has a positive effect on our peace with our enemies. In Matt 5:9 Jesus says, *"Blessed are the peacemakers, for they shall be called sons of God."* When we make an effort to maintain peace with those who are difficult to get along with, it reflects our relationship with God and brings glory to His name. So can prayer help us *enjoy* our peace that surpasses all understanding? The Bible says that we can have this peace if we *let the peace of God rule in [our] hearts* (Col 3:15). So how do we let the peace of God rule in our hearts?

Faith, hope, love, joy, peace: simple words yet so essential to the "abundant life" Jesus has to offer those who come to Him. Why are they so often in short supply in the lives of many Christians? Because they neglect two fundamental tools God provides for them. These tools? The Word of God and prayer! Folks, whenever you find yourself in a spiritual "slump," let these two avenues of communication with God be the key to energizing your faith! Fortifying your hope! Activating your love! Enhancing your joy! Enjoying your peace!

Restoring the basic elements of the abundant life found only in Christ is not a mystery: Receive the implanted Word of God! *Therefore lay aside all filthiness and overflow of wickedness, and receive with meekness the implanted word, which is able to save your souls* (Jas 1:21).

In the remainder of the book we will look at the pattern that God has given us to initiate and maximize revitalization so that he can bring revival to our congregations and transformation to our communities.

Chapter 3

Revival: Requirements for Revitalization

Then the Lord appeared to Solomon by night, and said
to him: "I have heard your prayer, and have chosen this
place for Myself as a house of sacrifice. When I shut up
heaven and there is no rain, or command the locusts to
devour the land, or send pestilence among My people,
if My people who are called by My name will humble
themselves, and pray and seek My face, and turn from
their wicked ways, then I will hear from heaven, and
will forgive their sin and heal their land. Now My eyes
will be open and My ears attentive to prayer made in
this place. For now I have chosen and sanctified this
house, that My name may be there forever; and My eyes
and My heart will be there perpetually.

—2 Chr 7:12-16

WHAT DISTINGUISHES A HEALTHY and vigorous church is the
demonstration of the power of God in the lives of its people. It
is the presence and power of God manifested in real and tangible
ways that influence our neighbors and our community. The proof
of the presence and power of God is in changed lives.

A church that is truly healthy and alive is a church that
is seeing people's lives transformed by the power of God. It is
a place where people are coming to know Jesus Christ as their

personal Savior and Lord and where they are growing in their faith and walking with Him. It is a place where people are being set free from sin and addiction, where they are finding healing and wholeness. It is a place where marriages and families are being strengthened and relationships restored.

A healthy church is a church that is making a difference in its community and in the world. It is a church impacting lives for eternity, full of the presence and power of God. Are we trusting and believing in God for our power and strength, or are we rather trusting in our own abilities? This is the question we must ask ourselves. If we are depending on our own strength, then we will ultimately fail. But if we are depending on the power of God, then we can do all things through Christ, who gives us strength (Phil 4:13).

What is the distinguishing mark of your church—unity or division? Are you united in your love for God and your desire to follow His will for your lives? Are you united in your commitment to reach out to your community and share the gospel with them? And are you united in your belief that the power of God can change lives? Or are there division and tensions among the people of the congregation? Are there cliques that form pockets of disunity? Are there individuals trying to get the upper hand on others?

What is the posture of the church that you serve—go and tell, or stay and protect? In other words, is your church focused on evangelism and discipleship or on maintaining the status quo? A healthy church will always have a focus on evangelism and discipleship, because that's what Jesus Christ has called us to do.

If we are unwilling to change and grow, then we will ultimately stagnate and die. But if we are open to change and willing to grow, then we will be a healthy and vibrant church that is full of the presence and power of God. We must understand that a church that needs revitalization is not destined for death and irrelevance but is positioned for possibilities and opportunities bringing glory to God. A church in need of revitalization has become comfortable with its current state and is no longer reaching people for Christ. It is a church that has lost its passion for evangelism and discipleship.

But it's not too late! Things can turn around, and the congregation can truly experience the life-changing power of God once again.

All we need is a renewal of our passion for God and a fresh infilling of the Holy Spirit. Then we will be able to reach people for Christ and impact our community for eternity. If we want to see a healthy and vibrant church, then we must be willing to put in the work. It takes time and effort to build relationships, to evangelize, and to disciple. But it is so worth it when we see people's lives transformed by the power of God. Are you up for the challenge?

If you are ready to experience the life-changing power of God, then take the first step and do what's needed to be a healthy and vibrant church today. You won't regret it! As Rick Warren said, "A healthy church is a church that is making a difference in its community and in the world."

As the body of Christ, we are called to be the hands and feet of Jesus. We are called to go into all the world and share the gospel with everyone we meet. We are called to love our neighbors as ourselves. We are called to be salt and light in a dark and lost world. Are you being the hands and feet of Jesus in your community? Are you sharing the gospel with those around you? Are you loving your neighbors as yourself? If not, then what are you waiting for? If you don't then what will be left is what Paul told Timothy, *They will turn their ears away from the truth, and be turned aside to fables* (2 Tim 4:4).

Many churches today have turned away from the truth of the gospel and have instead been turned to fables, believing the lie from the enemy that things are good enough. They no longer preach the gospel in its fullness but instead focus on feel-good messages that tickle people's ears. This is not the kind of church God wants us to be. He wants us to be a church founded on the truth of His Word and preaching the gospel in its fullness. Erwin McManus said, "The church is not a building; it's a living, breathing organism made up of people who are passionate about God and His mission."

Revitalization efforts and revival from God can only come if we are living our lives for Christ, having confidence in God's economy, and believing that the size of a church does not determine the effectiveness of the church in its community—but that God does!

Churches living for survival rather than in revival

Congregations in survival mode exist to maintain the status quo by doing things the way they've always been done. The problem with the status quo, or "business-as-usual," is that it's so comfortable and neutral that we often don't hear the loud alarm bells. All we hear is everything's fine. So how do you know if it's time to push for a change? The culture and society you're trying to reach are changing constantly (there's your alarm bell). The problem with status quo is that at one point "it worked." The methods your church is stuck in worked at some time. Because they worked, the church stayed with them—but for too long. The reason they worked was that through them the church was able to maintain its current state. The problem, however, is that things have changed, and if the church doesn't change with it, the church will become irrelevant. We change methods, approaches, and strategies for reaching the ear and hearts of people. We absolutely do not change the message of Jesus Christ. The message of the gospel stays the same.

The other problem with status quo is that it often leads to stagnation. When a church is stuck in its ways, it stops growing (alarm bell), becoming stagnant and failing to reach new people. This is a huge problem, because the church needs to be constantly growing and reaching new people with the gospel for new life and growth to come. If your church is stuck in the status quo, then it's time for a change. It's time to start reaching out to your community and sharing the gospel with them to be a church that is truly making a difference.

If your church leadership meetings are dominated by discussing financial issues like paying utility bills and how to get more money in the offering plate instead of reaching more people for Christ, then this is "church-centric" thinking. Such inward focus leads to decline. New people are not coming in, and the ones that are there aren't being discipled.

Another problem with an inward focus is that it can often lead to arrogance. When church people are focused on themselves, they can start to think that they're better than everyone else, looking down on other churches and denominations, believing they have all the answers and that everyone else is wrong. This is a dangerous place to be, because it leads to division within the body of Christ. I do not believe that they intend to have this type of thinking but it can start to creep in if not checked on a regular basis.

Churches living for revival

Churches living for revival exist to reach people for Christ, to see new people coming to know the Lord. They want to see lives changed by the power of the gospel and therefore are focused on evangelism and discipleship. These churches are making a difference in their communities and around the world because they see the people as individuals that Jesus came and died for. They see them as valuable and worth the time and effort to invest into them.

They have a mindset that is "kingdom-centric" and not just centered on themselves. They have a "revival fire" way of thinking, focused on others, seeing people the way that Jesus sees them—lost sheep in need of a shepherd. They have a burden for the lost and want to see them saved. These churches are being used by God to change lives and make a difference in the world.

Such forward-looking churches are not just getting by—they're thriving. They're seeing people saved and transformed by the power of the gospel, making disciples for Jesus Christ. These churches are on fire for God, and it is evident in everything they do. God is moving in ways that people are being healed, transformed, and released from bondage. The fetters of the enemy that had bound people for so many years are now broken and loosed.

Do you want to see your church thrive? Do you want to see your church making a difference in the world? Then It's time to make sure that the people of the church are seeking God with all their hearts, minds, and soul. It's time to pray for a fresh outpouring of the Holy Spirit. It's time to ask God to revive your church.

When we allow God to move in our churches, he will do amazing things. He will breathe new life into us, and we will be on fire for Him like never before. We will be used by Him to reach people in ways that we never thought possible. We will see lives changed and transformed by the power of the gospel. We will see our communities impacted for Christ. Churches that see true revival are growing and attract people because of what God is doing. The community is being impacted for Christ, and people's lives are being changed.

There is a stunning parallel in Acts regarding the simplicity of the lives of the believers and the power and effectiveness of their ministry. Real revival is evident through the outpouring of the Holy Spirit evidenced in the lives of our people. But the Acts church did not need revival because they were living in the overflow of the original outpouring of the Holy Spirit's presence and power. We, on the other hand, desperately need another touch from heaven.

The kind of revival we're seeking will not come through clever marketing or powerful preaching alone. It will come as we position ourselves for a fresh outpouring of the Holy Spirit in our individual lives and churches. We must be people who are yielded to Him and totally dependent upon Him if we are going to see the kind of revival that will change our world. That is what revitalization really is, putting ourselves in a place for God to pour upon us. It is worth repeating, revitalization is the intentional positioning of ourselves for the divine provision of revival.

If you are ready for your church to experience true revival, then begin praying and seeking God with all your heart. Prayer is the key to unlocking revival in our churches. When you allow God to move in your life, he will do amazing things. He will breathe new life into you and your church. He will use you to reach people in ways you never thought possible. You will see lives changed and transformed by the power of the gospel. You will see your community impacted for Christ.

Start praying today for a fresh outpouring of the Holy Spirit in your life and your church. Ask God to revive His people and to use your church to reach your community for Christ. Let us be a people who are passionate for His fire to ignite us and who are willing to pray and seek God with all our hearts.

Revival starts with revitalization

The purpose of revival is to restore us, the church, back to our original state of righteousness, authority, purpose, and power. We need to be reminded of who we are in Christ and what he has called us to do. We have strayed so far from our roots that we need to go back and revisit them. We need to allow the Holy Spirit to revive us and restore us to the people God originally intended us to be. We will be so impacted by the presence of God that we will no longer be content just to survive; we will be driven by a passion to live for Christ and to see His kingdom come. When we as the created come into a close contact with the Creator we are changed in a way that we cannot remain the same.

We could spend days on each of these topics, but I want to share some details about power in the church and the apparent lack of it. As noted earlier, many churches in America are in a state of descent, dried-up devotion, and trying to survive rather than be revived. A lack of power is the result. The early church had great power because they had a yielded lifestyle that allowed the Holy Spirit to work through them. We must have the same yielded lifestyle if we are going to see the power of God at work in our churches today. It must start with people that humble themselves before a holy God.

Churches are not demonstrating the manifest power of God because too many of our people are discouraged, disillusioned, disheartened, and discontented, trying to survive rather than to be revived. We've become a people who have more faith in our traditions than in the power of God. We need to be revived! Intentional positioning of ourselves so that the Holy Spirit can shape us, direct us, and mold us into the image of Christ.

There is no revival because . . .

People are walking around depressed, unhappy, and living as if there were no hope. This is because they have lost hope since they have forgotten who they are in Christ and what he has called them to do. We need to be reminded of our identity in Christ and our purpose for living. When we know who we are and what we are called to do, we will have hope. And when we have hope, we will be revived!

Outwardly people will at least try putting on a good face, but privately there is no power at all in them since they have given up and lost hope. In order to experience revival, we need to reevaluate our faith and put our trust in the power of God instead of our own abilities or manmade traditions. We need to be a people who are passionate for revival and are willing to pray and seek God with all our hearts.

Fewer and fewer people long, hunger, and thirst for God's power and presence since they are not being fed. They are not receiving the Word of God on a regular basis. They are not pulling themselves up to the table and feasting on the bounty that God has prepared and placed before them. They are not being challenged to grow spiritually. Instead, they are being spoon-fed a diet of entertainment and fluff that leaves them malnourished and unfulfilled. If we are going to experience revival, we need to seek out sound teaching that will challenge us to grow spiritually. We need to be passionate for revival and willing to pray and seek God with all our hearts.

Another reason we see so many in the survival-only mode is that they have become complacent. They have become comfortable in their sin and no longer see the need for change. They have allowed their churches to become safe havens for sinners rather than altars of repentance. We absolutely want people that do not know Jesus to come and experience the freedom of salvation, but the sin must be dealt with once someone comes into the saving knowledge of the Savior. If we're going to experience revival, we need to repent of our complacency and take up the mantle of revival. Clutching onto the salvation and freedom that Jesus provides and to release and turn from intentional and known sin that entangles us.

Lack of righteousness and holiness is another impediment to revival. God cannot and will not be part of the sin that too many people still live in. The reason we don't have more power is that we have quenched and grieved the Holy Spirit by living in disobedience, unforgiveness, and impurity. We need to repent of our sin and turn back to Him with all our hearts. Known sin in the church must be addressed for God to be able to bless and honor that church.

The church may talk about the day that God will come and pour out revival somewhere, sometime in the future. Some may talk about the "good old days" when God's presence seemed to be so powerful. Where is the present-tense reality of His manifest presence right here, right now? Do you long for more of God? Are you hungry for His presence? Do you thirst for His power? Then take up the mantle of revival and pray that God will send revival to His church!

Unity, prayer, worship, and a broken and contrite spirit help prepare us for and can welcome in the presence of the Lord. As we read in 2 Chr 7:14, *If My people who are called by My name will humble themselves, and pray and seek My face, and turn from their wicked ways, then I will hear from heaven, and will forgive their sin and heal their land.* There must be a *remember, recognize, repent,* and *return* before we can go from survival to revival.

1. We must remember who we are in Christ: we are a
   people who are called by His name and have been
   given the authority to change our world!

2. We must recognize and acknowledge our waywardness.

3. We must repent of our sin and turn back to God with
   all our hearts.

4. We must return to Him with all of our hearts, minds,
   and strength.

As noted before, prayer is essential if we want to see the power of God at work in our churches. What would it look like if your church were on fire for God? If revival began in your church, what would be the consequences? Would people be saved? Would lives be changed? Would families be healed? Would marriages be restored? Would addictions be broken? These are just a few of the things that could happen if revival came to your church. But it all starts with prayer.

Believing and obeying God are essential for His moving on His people. There cannot be revival until people are fully trusting and believing God for all their needs. We also need to be careful not just to go through the motions of doing things for God but to make sure that our hearts are truly in it. Revival will come when we passionately seek after God with all our hearts!

In order for us to experience revitalization, we need to be people who believe that God is powerful enough to work mightily in and through our lives. Do you believe he can use you and your church to change your world? The key to unlocking the power of God is faith. When we have faith, we can see needs met. We can also see how God can use us to meet those needs.

When God's presence ceases to be a tangible reality in a church, spiritual life cannot be sustained for long. A church that is not being renewed by the Spirit of God will soon become a dead church. A church without revival is a dying church. But a church full of the presence of God is a thriving church!

Churches need to be places where people can encounter the presence of God. But unfortunately, many churches have become places where the presence of God is no longer felt. This is because they have lost touch with the things that sustain His presence. The only way to keep the presence of God in our churches is for transformation to take place. We need a fresh touch from God! It needs to be a church where people are finding deliverance. Set free from the clutches of sin that binds them. New converts to the faith. Baptisms as a testimony of people dying to self and being raised in new life in Jesus Christ. And a healthy church is one that has solid steps for discipleship of not only the new believers but for maturity of all believers.

There must be an unapologetic faith to read and respond to God's Word. God expects us to understand and know His commandments. We need to be doers of the word and not just hearers only. Can you only imagine the power and hope that living out in our lives what the word of God has to say for us.

We need to be careful that we don't get so caught up in doing things for God that we forget actually to spend time with Him. It's easy to get busy with the business of church and neglect communing with God. We need to make sure we're taking time out to be still and know that he is God.

For a church that is moving from surviving to reviving, worship must flow from a heart that is bent toward praise, glory, and honor to the one true King. God said that he inhabits the praises of His people. When we worship God with all our hearts, minds, and strength, we're inviting Him to come and dwell in our midst.

When we yielded our lives to Christ, we became new creations. The old things passed away and everything became new! We become new creatures in Christ! We are transformed by the power of the Holy Spirit and begin walking in newness of life.

Revitalization and revival facilitates lives being transformed and restored to the "image of God." God's heart is for His people to be conformed into the image of His Son. When we see people coming to Christ and being changed by the power of the Holy Spirit, we are seeing God's word being lived out in flesh.

What is the distinguishing mark of our church—unity or division?

There is no revival because . . . lack of unity in the church body. The church is supposed to be a place of unity, but unfortunately it is often a place of division. Division in the church hinders the work of God and quenches the Spirit. Revival cannot take place in an environment of division. We need to come together in unity if we are going to see transformation in our churches.

The church is not a building; it is a people. And when the people of God are united, we can see the power of God at work in mighty ways! When the church is divided, it is powerless. The enemy loves to see division in the church because it weakens our testimony and hinders our effectiveness.

Power comes through unity. Acts 2:43–44 tells us, *Then fear came upon every soul, and many wonders and signs were done through the apostles. Now all who believed were together, and had all things in common.* We need to put aside our differences and come together as one body. Only then will we be able to see the power of God at work in mighty ways.

There are too many sections in the church. Sections, divisions, clichés don't exist in the church model formed by Jesus. Unity comes from a heart that has love for others as Jesus commanded. *Love never fails* (1 Cor 13:8).

Unity of the church represents the unity of the Trinity, of the gospel message and the furtherance of the kingdom. Division occurs when there are elements of "self" creeping into the body of believers and in offices of leadership. Jesus Himself said that a house divided cannot stand. Where gospel priority and importance once stood, now alternative worldviews dominate. We are warned about individuals that would come into the church and try to sway the power and control of the church through division.

The church has become a marketplace of religious goods and services instead of being *the pillar and ground of the truth* (1 Tim 3:15). When the church is no longer about Christ and His gospel but about various programs that entice people to come, division is inevitable.

What is the one thing that can bring the church together and produce unity? The answer is simple: the gospel! When we preach Christ and Him crucified, when we lift up Jesus as Lord and Savior, the Holy Spirit will do His work.

In conclusion, the church desperately needs the Holy Spirit to be the guide in all things. We need to seek the face of God and ask Him to pour out His Spirit on us. We need to cry out for a fresh touch from God. We need to come together in unity and love one another as Christ has commanded us.

If the church is the very representation of Christ, then unity is the dominating characteristic of the body of believers. Jesus Himself prayed that unity would be what anyone would see in His disciples: *"That they may all be one, as You, Father, are in Me, and I in You; that they also may be one in Us . . . I in them, and You in Me; that they may be made perfect in one"* (John 17:21, 23).

Contrasting the unity that Christ died to establish is the division sown by the adversary as part of his "divide and conquer" strategy. *Every kingdom divided against itself is brought to desolation, and every city or house divided against itself will not stand* (Matt 12:25). Why would anyone think that the church could be an exception to this principle? If disunity is the result of human nature left to its own devices, then it should come as no surprise that carnality would rear its ugly head in the church.

The key to maintaining unity is love. When we allow the love of God to flow through us, it will be impossible to stay divided. The apostle Paul gives a strong admonition against division in 1 Cor 3:1–9:

> I, brethren, could not speak to you as to spiritual people but as to carnal, as to babes in Christ. I fed you with milk and not with solid food; for until now you were not able to receive it, and even now you are still not able; for you are still carnal. For where there are envy, strife, and divisions among you, are you not carnal and behaving like mere men? For when one says, "I am of Paul," and another, "I am of Apollos," are you not carnal? Who then is Paul, and who is Apollos, but ministers through whom you believed, as the Lord gave to each one? I planted, Apollos watered, but God gave the increase. So then neither he who plants is anything, nor he who waters, but God who gives the increase. Now he who plants and he who waters are one, and each one will receive his own reward according to his own labor. For we are God's fellow workers; you are God's field, you are God's building.

In this passage Paul is addressing the issue of division in the church at Corinth. There were two main factions in the church—those who followed Paul and those who followed Apollos. Paul is clear that this division was not of God but rather was due to the fleshly nature of the people. He goes on to say that neither Paul nor Apollos was anything—it was only God who caused the growth. This is an important principle for us to understand. When we allow division to occur in the church, we are hindering the work of God. We are quenching the Spirit.

What is the posture of your church? "Go and tell" or "Stay and protect"?

There is no renewal because—there is no action. The American church has become a stagnant pool. The call of God is to "go and tell," but we have instead decided to "stay and protect." We have become content with just maintaining the status quo. We have lost our missional focus and become inwardly focused. We need to remember that the Great Commission is not an option—it is a command. We are called to go into all the world and preach the gospel. When we do, people will be saved and the church will be revitalized.

We must take action if we want to see revival in our churches. It starts with each individual Christian taking seriously the call to be fishers of men. We need to be sharing our faith with those who are lost. We need to be inviting them to church. We need to be living our lives in such a way that people can see Christ in us. When we do these things, we will begin to see revival in our churches. Revival is not something that just happens—it is something we must put effort toward through our revitalization efforts. Some would argue against such statements but God Himself said that "If my people who are called by my name will humble themselves. That means we have a role to play in this move of God.

The requirements for revitalization include—

1. A vision from God

2. A willingness to take action

3. A passion for lost people

4. A commitment to holiness

5. A reliance on the power of the Holy Spirit.

The truth is that the world does not want our religion. The truth is not in our church culture or becoming one of our statistics (counting noses). But many people will respond to God's love genuinely expressed through His people who carry the fragrance of Christ to a world who does not know Him. *And they went out and preached everywhere, the Lord working with them and confirming the word through the accompanying signs* (Mark 16:20). The gospel is still the power of God for salvation to everyone who believes (Rom 1:16).

The early church was a vital, growing, relevant community of Jesus followers who turned their world upside down. We must become that church again if we want to see revival. Revival will not come through programs or the latest fads—it will come when we allow God to work through us. When we are obedient to His call, he will do the work of revival in our churches. All we need to do is be willing to take action.

When God's presence ceases to be a tangible reality in a church, spiritual life cannot be sustained for long. When God's presence begins to recede from a church, the goodness, His light, and His life begin to grow fainter and darkness begins to increase and take hold. The Jesus life can hardly survive where the sense of God's presence is so dim.

A. W. Tozer wrote, "What comes into our minds when we think about God is the most important thing about us."[1] If we're going to see the life of Christ in our churches, we must first have a vision from God. We must see Him for who he is—the Almighty, all-powerful, all-knowing, all-loving God. We must see Him as holy and perfect. And we must see ourselves as sinners in need of His saving grace and forgiveness.

When we have a right view of God, we will be willing to take action. We will be motivated by His love to share the gospel with

1. Tozer, *Knowledge of the Holy*, 1.

those who are lost. We will be passionate about seeing people come to Christ and experience the life-changing power of the Holy Spirit. We will be committed to holiness, because we want to please God in all we do. And we will rely on the Holy Spirit to work through us, because we know that we can do nothing without Him.

What happens is that the people of God slowly become desensitized to the loss of His presence and to the growing darkness around them. As a result, hearts become hardened, senses are dulled, and perspective is lost. The church falls into survival rather than revival. To counter this, we must have a vision from God—a clear understanding of who he is and who we are in relation to Him.

When we take action and invite the lost into our churches, something amazing happens. We begin seeing life to spring up where dry bones lay before. People are saved and transformed by the power of the Holy Spirit. Lives are changed forever. And the church is revitalized.

The only solution from being powerless is to run after and pursue God, being unified as the body, putting away all the things that do not look like Christ, engaging in prayer that is desperate and sincere for the heart of God, placing all the elements together in action, putting the hands and feet and heart of Christ to work in a tangible way. It is then that the church can turn from survival to revival.

It's time to take action. It's time for new life!

Chapter 4

Remember: Whose Kingdom Are We Building?

Thus says the Lord:

"What injustice have your fathers found in Me, that they have gone far from Me, have followed idols, and have become idolaters? Neither did they say, 'Where is the Lord, Who brought us up out of the land of Egypt, Who led us through the wilderness, through a land of deserts and pits, through a land of drought and the shadow of death, through a land that no one crossed and where no one dwelt?' I brought you into a bountiful country, to eat its fruit and its goodness. But when you entered, you defiled My land and made My heritage an abomination. The priests did not say, 'Where is the Lord?' And those who handle the law did not know Me; the rulers also transgressed against Me; The prophets prophesied by Baal, and walked after things that do not profit."

—Jer 2:5-8

Churches often become inwardly focused, trying to build their own kingdom instead of God's. As pastors and church revitalizers, we know it's important to remember whose kingdom we're really building. Are we trying to advance God's kingdom or our own? To make sure our efforts are in line with God's desires, we need to constantly be reminded of what the Bible says about His plans for us. As we read and reflect on scripture, may we be guided by the Holy Spirit in all we do as we serve Him and His church.

If we're honest, most of us would have to admit that we often build our lives and ministries around our own kingdom goals. We can be so busy achieving our own objectives that we unknowingly leave God out of the picture. Being distracted by trying to gain more in attendance, seeking recognition for ministry efforts that have gone well for us, or that pat on the back by another ministry leader. But Jesus said, *"Seek first the kingdom of God"* (Matt 6:33).

Understand that everything belongs to God and that it is His kingdom that everything is to be done for and not our own. What does it mean to build God's kingdom? It means living a life focused on glorifying God and making Him known to others. It means being obedient to His Word and His will for our lives. It means sacrificially serving others and meeting needs. It also means doing the right thing even when no one else is looking.

When it comes to serving God, there are two common mistakes Christians make. The first is trying to build our own kingdom instead of God's. The second is not building anything at all since it's all God's.

There's certainly nothing wrong with having goals and dreams. In fact, God often gives us specific goals to accomplish for His kingdom. But we need to make sure that our goals are in line with His kingdom purposes. We also need to be careful that our pursuit of these goals doesn't become an idol in our lives. Idols can take many different forms. They could be a career, a relationship, a possession, or even a good cause that we're passionate about. If we're not careful, anything can become an idol if we allow it to take the place of God in our lives. The key is to keep our eyes on Jesus and make sure that he is our number-one priority. When we do that, everything else will fall into place.

So whose kingdom are you building—God's or yours? Take some time to think about that today. And ask God to help you keep your priorities in line with His kingdom purposes. What has caused the *why* we do ministry to change to *how well we do that ministry*? Today it seems that the focus has shifted from *why* we do something to how we do it. We are so focused on the methods and the means that we often forget about the end goal. This can be seen in many different areas of life, including our faith.

Remember that it's easy to let the "doing" distract us from the "reason" for our doing in the first place. Let's keep our eyes on the prize and focus on building God's kingdom instead of our own. Think about a time when you got caught up in the *doing* and lost sight of the *why*. What was the result? How could you have avoided that situation? Spend some time today asking God to help you keep your eyes on Him and His kingdom purposes. *Seek first the kingdom of God and His righteousness, and all these things shall be added to you* (Matt 6:33). Our goal is to glorify God and to enjoy Him forever. Everything else will fall into place when we keep this in mind.

Where do your priorities lie? Isn't it true that when we focus on our goals and objectives, everything else falls into place? How can you make sure that God's kingdom is first in your life? One way is to set aside time each day to pray and seek His guidance. Another way is to be intentional about serving others and sharing the gospel.

Revitalization requires our remembering the "why"

> Is it time for you yourselves to dwell in your paneled houses, and this temple to lie in ruins?
>
> —HAG 1:4

The dream was coming true. The time had come for the exiled people to return from Babylon, their place of captivity. Zerubbabel brought the first wave of Israelites back to Jerusalem. They were tasked with building the temple of the Lord, and the excitement was more than they could contain. But the ticking of time can be an enemy for the mission. This is because with time comes complacency. We know the reason the Lord spoke the rebuke to the people about the fact that they had stopped working on the temple and living in houses finer than what the Lord Himself had. Because of opposition, resistance, and distractions, the people had turned to building for themselves instead of for the Lord. The enemy will do everything in his power to distract you from the Lords work.

The question posed by Haggai to the people is a question for us today: Is this a time for you yourselves to dwell in your paneled houses while His house lies in ruins? The answer is an emphatic *no*! We are to be about the business of the Lord. We are to be about His mission. We are not to be focused on our own personal agendas but rather on building His kingdom.

What is your motivation? It should be to glorify God and to enjoy Him forever. We can make all this a lot easier if we remember that. Look at the times we live in now. There is probably no greater time as now, full of things that pull our attention away from the Lord's work and His service. We can be easily sidetracked and end up neglecting the most important thing—building God's kingdom. It seems that everything in the world is calling for our attention. So let us be intentional about keeping our eyes on Jesus.

We run from one place to another checking off things to do and places to be, tempted to lose sight of *why* we do things because of our overwhelming concern for *how* we do them. Amid our doing, we need to remember that it is not about us or our abilities. It's about God and His mission. When we keep this perspective, everything else dims in comparison.

In our daily lives, numerous pressures, demands, expectations and tasks push in to all sides of our lives. *Do this, Be there, Finish that, Call them*—it seems as though everyone wants something from us, and soon there is little left to give as we run out of all our energy and time. We can get to the point at which we feel as if we're running on empty and just going through the motions. It is at these times that we need to remember our *why*.

Our values and priorities are reflected in how we use our resources—time, money, strength, and talent. Often our actions make little of our words. We say God is number one in our lives, but then we neglect Him to a lesser number of "to do" lists in our lives. We need to be honest with ourselves and check our priorities. Are they really in the order we claim?

Time is one of our most precious resources and it is given to us by God. How we use our time reflects what we value in life. If we want to make God a priority in our lives, we need to use our time wisely, which we can do by scheduling time for things that are important to our relationship with the Lord, like spending time with Him, family, and friends. When we use our time wisely, much can be done for the kingdom. Many times kingdom building is build off of relationship that we have taken the time to foster with others.

Money is another resource we have been given by God. How we use our money reflects what we value in life. If we want to make God a priority in our lives, we need to be wise with our money by giving generously to the Lord's work and being good stewards of all His resources.

Our strength and talents are also resources that have been given to us by God. How we use our strength and talents reflects what we value in life, and we need to use them for His glory. We can do this by using our gifts and talents to serve others and build His kingdom. Being the reflection of Jesus to others.

When we keep our eyes on Jesus and make Him our priority, everything else will line up as it should. We need to be intentional about spending time with God, using our resources wisely, and serving others with our gifts and talents.

Even in the church, work itself can be a distraction from the original purposes of God. We can get so caught up in the "ministry" that we forget why we're doing it. We can be so focused on the program that we no longer see people as God's children but simply as projects. It is important to keep our eyes on Jesus in all aspects of our lives, including our work in the church. Not forgetting that every soul is valuable to Jesus because he came, died, and raised again for them.

There will always be things vying for our attention and time. It's up to us to decide what is most important. Our problem is not the volume of demands or lack of scheduling skills, but values, what is profoundly important to us. If we neglect the important things in life, we will never have time for them. It is our values that will determine what we do with our time.

Whose kingdom are we building? God's or ours?

Our attention shifts from the original purpose to the increasing desire to grow the church while forgetting that it all starts with and belongs to God. Oh, we start well, as did the workers for the temple, building for the kingdom of God and His glory, but distractions get in the way because things are going well and growth has come. If we are not careful, success can distract us from glorifying God, to thinking that we did something in our own efforts. It can make us a little too big for our britches. We take our eyes off Jesus and begin thinking more highly of ourselves. It becomes "my church" or "my congregation." We get puffed up with pride and begin thinking that we're responsible for the growth, not God. We lose sight of who is really in control. When this happens, we need to repent and ask God to forgive us. We need to get our priorities straight and put Jesus back in His rightful place as Lord and Savior. We need to focus on His kingdom and not our own.

If we're not careful, success can become an enemy to the work of ministry. It's exciting since people are coming in and finances are not as much of a problem as before. This is where we must be careful, because the good things and the shiny things become our gods as we take our eyes off the original and true purpose, our kingdom purpose.

It's time that we ask ourselves some hard questions. Whose kingdom are we building, God's or ours? What is our motivation? Are we in it for the glory of God or the recognition and accolades of man? These are tough questions, but they must be asked. We need to keep our eyes on Jesus, the author and finisher of our faith. If we do, we will not be led astray by success or anything else. Success can lead to being comfortable and complacent which can head to status-quo. These elements if left unchecked can head a church into the need for revitalization.

Remember Jesus's words in Matt 6:19–21: *"Do not lay up for yourselves treasures on earth, where moth and rust destroy and where thieves break in and steal; but lay up for yourselves treasures in heaven, where neither moth nor rust destroys and where thieves do not break in and steal. For where your treasure is, there your heart will be also."*

What has caused the "why" to change to "how"?

In our desire to see our church grow, we can easily get caught up in the numbers game. How many people attend? How much money do we take in? How many programs do we offer? We can get so focused on these things that we forget why we are doing them. We can get so consumed with the task that we forget the purpose. The purpose of the church is to glorify God, not ourselves. The church is not about us—it's about Him. It's not about numbers or finances; it's about obedience and faithfulness. When we lose sight of this, we can easily focused on trying to grow our own kingdoms instead of God's. We are merely stewards of what he has entrusted to us. Our job is to be obedient and faithful, not successful. If we focus on these things, the numbers will take care of themselves. Success comes by be obedient to Jesus and His word. Jesus said, *I will build My church (Matt. 16:18).* He takes all the weight off us to be responsible for the outcomes. Jesus will be the one to build and grow the church through our faithful obedience.

Often people start off strong and energetic for the work of the kingdom, but then trouble comes along. Disgruntled bystanders, ones that are not doing the work, deflate the enthusiasm that the people have had for the work. The work then becomes a burden because the focus has changed from Jesus to the people who are not helping. This is where repentance and refocusing need to happen so that the church can get back on track. The key is to keep our eyes on Jesus. The nay-sayers are usually not the ones doing the work. They point and pick with every effort that is underway but this is another distraction the enemy uses.

At the time when Haggai encouraged the people to finished rebuilding the temple, opposition from hostile neighbors had caused them to feel discouraged and to neglect the temple, thus neglecting God Himself. But Haggai's message turned them around and motivated them to pick up their tools and continue the work they had begun.

The key for us is to keep our eyes on Jesus. Let us not get discouraged and give up when the going gets tough. Let us press on and finish the work he has called us to do.

Priorities—God or money?

We can go about and build a kingdom of possessions and amass all the wealth that we can possibly imagine, but that will not do us any good when the end of days come to each one of us on earth. Jesus said that we cannot serve two masters, and if we try to, then we will love the one and despise the other. You cannot serve both God and money. How often do you find yourself consumed with thoughts of things you want or things you must do? We can get so focused on our own lives and our own desires that we forget about God and the bigger picture. We are merely stewards of what he has entrusted to us.

We are living in a temporal world surrounded by temporal things. The things of this world will all fade away, but the things of God will last forever. Let us be obedient and faithful stewards of what he has entrusted to us. And let us not get discouraged when the going gets tough but press on and finish the race.

The kingdom that is taking all your time, energy, and effort is the kingdom that will drive your life. But remembering that this life is only for a little while and that the things we collect and hold dear will be in somebody else's hands or in a rummage sale or dumpster someday. It is our relationship with Jesus that will last forever. So let's focus on building that instead of our own little kingdoms.

When we keep our eyes on Jesus and make His kingdom our priority, he will take care of the rest. We don't need to worry about the things of this world; he will take care of us. We can trust God to provide for us because he is a good and faithful Father. Let us fix our eyes on Jesus and not get sidetracked by the things of this world. And let us remember that this life is only temporary, but our relationship with Him is eternal.

The kingdom of God is eternal. The kingdom that we as His children, heirs with Christ, inherit and in which we're to be workers is an everlasting kingdom. *Your kingdom is an everlasting kingdom, And Your dominion endures throughout all generations* (Ps 145:13). In this life our focus should not be on temporal things but on things that have eternal value. We are to build the kingdom of God by making disciples of all nations, teaching them to observe all things Jesus has commanded us (Matt 28:18–20).

It can become so easy to let the good work and successful work to start glorifying you and your congregation rather than glorifying God. Members can start to think they did it through their good efforts and the kingdom shift begins. When we let our success go to our heads, it is a sign that we have lost sight of who is really in charge. The church is not about us; it is about Him. It is not about numbers or finances; it is about obedience and faithfulness.

Eliminating distractions from the work of the kingdom is important to keeping on task and on mission. The more time that passes, more opposition will arise, and resistance will begin to gain ground and pull you from the focus, which is the furtherance of the kingdom of God.

Five Ways to Build for Kingdom Growth

1. **Pray for guidance from the Holy Spirit in all you do in building the kingdom.** The kingdom belongs to God, and he will direct you in the work. Building for the kingdom can involve many different activities, such as evangelism, discipleship, serving others, and more. It is important to be led by the Holy Spirit in all you do so that you can be sure you're doing

what God wants you to do. Trusting in God and following His guidance will lead to the best results in building His kingdom. *Trust in the Lord with all your heart, and lean not on your own understanding; In all your ways acknowledge Him, and He shall direct your paths* (Prov 3:5–6).

2. **Make disciples.** *"Make disciples of all the nations . . . teaching them to observe all things that I have commanded you"* (Matt 28:19–20). There is no more foundational way to build the kingdom of God than by making disciples who make disciples who make disciples. Telling others about Christ is the only way to build the kingdom. We must be unashamed and bold in proclaiming the gospel to anyone that will listen.

3. **Honor God with your time, talent, and treasure.** In order to build God's kingdom, we need to use our time, talent, and treasure to honor Him. This means using our time wisely, using our talents to serve others, and giving generously. We need to be careful with how we spend our time, because it is a precious commodity. We should also be careful with how we use our talents, because they are gifts from God that we should use to bless others. Finally, we need to be generous with our treasure, because it is an expression of our love for God. When we use our time, talent, and treasure to honor God, we are truly building His kingdom.

4. **Obey Jesus's commands and be faithful in doing His will.** To build the kingdom of God, we must obey Jesus's commands and be faithful in doing His will. This means living according to His Word and being obedient to His laws. It also means being a witness for Him, telling others about His love and forgiveness. Additionally, it means showing kindness and compassion to those in need and being peacemakers in our homes, workplaces, and communities. Finally, it means being faithful stewards of all that God has entrusted to us. When we live out these things, we are building the kingdom of God on earth as it is in heaven.

5. **Share the gospel with those who don't know Him.** Our church has been built upon the foundation of sharing the gospel with those who do not yet know Christ. Our goal is to reach everyone around us so that they might hear about the eternal life offered through Jesus Christ.

Although this work is difficult and there are many obstacles in our way, God has given us His promise that we can build His kingdom—if only we choose to put Him first. With Jesus's leadership and the power of prayer behind us, we will succeed at building His kingdom by sharing the gospel with those who don't know Him.

These are things we can do to build God's kingdom rather than our own. When we focus on building His kingdom, he will be glorified, and we will be blessed. Let us not get sidetracked by the things of this world but keep our eyes on Jesus and His everlasting kingdom.

Satan seeks to distract us from building God's kingdom by offering wealth and fame. These things are not bad in themselves, but they can become idols when we worship them or put too much importance on them. We need to remember that this world will pass away (1 John 2:17) and focus our efforts instead on what lasts forever—our relationship with Jesus Christ and helping to spread the gospel.

There are many ways we can contribute to God's work so that His name is glorified here on earth. One way is through acts of kindness in which we help others without expecting anything in return. In Matt 25:40 Jesus said, *"Assuredly, I say to you, inasmuch as you did it to one of the least of these My brethren, you did it to Me."* If we want to build God's kingdom and bring Him glory right now, let us reach out and love others in practical ways.

Chapter 5

Recognize: Seeing What Is around You

Do you not say, 'There are still four months and then comes the harvest'? Behold, I say to you, lift up your eyes and look at the fields, for they are already white for harvest!

—John 4:35

How do we see the church that we serve and worship in? The answer may seem obvious—through our eyes, of course! But have you ever thought about how we *actually* see the church? Consider these three ways:

1. **Physically.** This is the most obvious way. We see the building, the people, and all the physical aspects of the church. As Christians we often think of the church as being an actual building, where believers gather to worship and receive instruction from God's Word. This is a true description of the church and how we view it. People also see the building as a place to go to get answers.

2. **Emotionally.** This is how we feel about the church. Do we have positive or negative emotions toward it? Emotional attachment to a church is very common for people who attended at a young age. Couples who were married in a church or loved ones now deceased who attended a particular church often have strong emotional ties to it.

3. **Spiritually.** This is the least obvious way but arguably the most important. When we see the church spiritually, we view it through the eyes of faith. We see it as a place where God dwells and where His people come to worship Him.

Regardless of how we see the church, it's important to remember that it's not just a building. The church consists of the people who make up the body of Christ. And each one of us has an important role to play in making it what it's meant to be.

What is your church like? What does it look like to you? Take a few moments to think about how you see your church. Is it a physical place, an emotional community, or a spiritual body of believers? How do you see the church that you serve and worship in? It is the place that people come to when seeking answers to questions and in times of trouble? It's a source of strength and comfort for many. It's also a community of believers who are committed to living out their faith in Christ. The church is all these things and more. But most importantly, the church is the body of Christ, and each one of us has a role to play in making it what it's meant to be.

Through what lens do you see your community? What is it you see when you look at the neighbors around you? If you were to take a good, hard look at your community through the eyes of faith, what would you see? Do you see people who are lost and in need of a Savior? Do you see people who are hurting and in need of comfort? Do you see people who are searching for answers to life's big questions? Do you see a run-down neighborhood that's drug infested and full of people who drain resources? Or do you see something else entirely?

How do you see yourself in ministry opportunities in the church and community? Do you see yourself as a minister of the gospel? This is an important role that each one of us must play in making the church what it's supposed to be. Or do you see yourself as a member of the community who just happens to go to church? This is an important perspective to have as well. The church is a community of believers who come together to worship and serve God. Regardless of what lens you see the church through, it's important to remember that each one of us has an important role to play in making the church what it's supposed to be.

For church revitalization to be effective, the existing congregation must have a clear understanding that their church is a place of opportunity and a mission station. They need to be reminded that their primary purpose is not simply to maintain the status quo but to reach out and share the gospel with those who are lost. This means being open to change and willing to try new things. It also means being willing to sacrifice their own comfort for the sake of the kingdom.

Are you willing to do what it takes to see your church revived?

All too often churches that need revitalization are seen as places of death and despair. But this doesn't have to be the case! If we change the way we see these churches, we can begin seeing them as places of hope and opportunity, as mission stations where the gospel can be proclaimed and lives can be transformed. But it starts with us. It requires much more than just showing up on Sunday mornings; it requires complete surrender of our lives to Christ and a commitment to follow His leading day in and day out.

The church may not always be perfect, but it's still the hope of the world. So if you are willing to do what it takes to see your church revived and thriving, then let God use you as His instrument in making it happen. And know that he has great plans for your community, plans that can be fulfilled only with a church full of believers who are committed to walking with Jesus every step of the way. Let's work together toward seeing our churches revived and striving toward their God-given purpose!

Seeing the community that you live in as
a "field ready for harvest" for God

The community you live in is not just a place to exist but also a place where God can use you to make a difference. It's a "field ready for harvest" for the gospel. This means that there are people all around you who are lost and in need of a Savior. And as noted earlier, it's your job to reach out and share the good news of Jesus Christ with them.

But what does this look like? It looks like being involved in your community. It looks like getting to know your neighbors and building relationships with them. It looks like serving others and meeting their needs. It looks like being a light in the darkness and sharing the hope that you have in Christ. It all starts with you. You must be willing to see your community through the eyes of faith and to believe that God can use you to make a difference. Are you ready to take up the challenge?

The church is a place where broken people can be healed and lost people can be found. It is a place of hope and of second chances. So no matter how imperfect it may be, the church is still worth fighting for. It is worth sacrificing for. It is worth dying for.

We live in a fallen world, where sin and death reign. Our churches are not immune to this reality. In fact, the church is often one of the places where we see the effects of sin and death most clearly. But despite all this, God still has a plan for His church. He intends to use it as a tool for bring about redemption and restoration in the world.

In order to see our churches revived, we must first see them as he intends to use them—as agents of change in a broken and fallen world. If you are willing to do what it takes to see your church revived and thriving, then let God use you as His instrument in making this happen. And know that he has great plans for your community—plans that can be fulfilled only with a church full of believers who are committed to seeing the way Jesus sees.

We must see our churches
through the lens of eternity.

We must see that the church is an eternal result of Christ's work putting together a body to represent and do the work here on earth that he started. There are eternal consequences to the work that we do. We must be committed to the message and the understanding of who we are as the church—an arm for Christ doing what he would do if he were still here physically. There is no greater honor than having God call you to lead His church, to serve Him through others. You hold a position of accountability, which means you will have critics and naysayers; but let those things be motivation for you to stand firm and work hard to do all that God has called you to fulfill so that in your final account before God, he sees that it is finished, that you did everything he asked of you for His glory!

We must see our churches as places
of hope and opportunity.

Churches are not to be seen as reservoirs of lostness or places that have no relevance in our community. Our churches are to be places of light and life where the hope of the gospel is made known.

To see our churches this way, we must first understand what God's pattern for revitalization looks like. This pattern is one where he uses His people to bring about change. It begins with prayer and repentance. We must humble ourselves before God and ask Him to search our hearts. We must confess our sins and turn from our wicked ways. Only then can we begin to see our churches the way God intends us to see them.

Next, we must share the gospel with those who are lost. We must point people to the hope that is found in Jesus Christ. We cannot be silent about our faith or shy away from sharing with others, regardless of their backgrounds or status. By loving those who are lost and letting them know how much we care for them, we will bring about true revitalization within our churches.

Finally, it's time to take action! When God calls us to do something, it's important that we act immediately and not wait around for things to happen on their own. When he calls us to share His love and truth with those who need it most, then it's essential that we get up and follow through by starting new ministry projects or volunteering at church events. Only then can we begin seeing real change within our churches.

If we want to see our churches revitalized, then we must be willing to put in the work. It starts with each one of us doing his or her part to follow God's pattern for change.

We must be willing to do what it takes to see our church revived.

We can make all the excuses in the world about why we haven't done something yet. The fact is, if we don't make a move, nothing will happen. It's God's pattern for revitalization that we make the first move. Once we do, he will honor our commitment and begin working through us to see His church revived.

In making the first move there are a few things we can do. First, we can start praying for revival. This may seem like a small thing, but it's essential. Revival begins with prayer. As we pray, we're asking God to do something that only he can do. Second, we can take practical steps toward revitalizing our church. This might mean anything from hosting discussions about how to improve our services to attending conferences and workshops on church revitalization. Whatever it takes, we must be willing to put in the time and energy if we want to see our churches revived. Ultimately, the key is that we are committed to seeing our church revived no matter what it takes. With God's help, nothing will stand in our way or stop us from achieving this goal. Let's devote ourselves wholeheartedly to this important task so that God's work through His church will continue to flourish throughout the world.

Too often I talk with other pastors that want revitalization in their church and see new growth and bigger ministries but there is one prominent problem with most that I talk to, they are not looking to put the work in, they just want a quick fix. They are looking for a silver bullet. Let me state this as clear and as plain as possible, its not going to happen without the work!

We must be involved in our community.

Part of the reason that your church needs revived is because the congregation has closed in on itself, looking after only its own concerns and interest, being church-centric and not kingdom-centric. If you want your church truly to be used by God, then you have to be intentional about seeking and serving those who are not a part of the church. You need to be relevant to your community and meet the needs that exist outside your church's walls.

When was the last time your church had a community event, something that would draw in those who don't normally darken the door of a church? When was the last time your church went on a mission trip or sent out a short-term mission team? Are you doing anything to reach those who are far from God? Do you see your church the way God sees it, as His instrument for bringing hope and healing to a lost and broken world? If not, then it's time for a change. It's time to start seeing your church the way God intends to use it.

We must see our community
through the eyes of faith.

Seeing our community as Jesus sees it, people who are lost without a shepherd, should be our goal. The church is a place where the hurting, the lost and searching, can find hope. It's the people who come together for worship, fellowship, and service. It is the body of Christ in action.

The church must be a hospital for sinners, not a museum for saints. It must ever keep before it the great commission that our Lord has given to His followers: *"Go into all the world and preach the gospel to every creature"* (Mark 16:15). The church exists for evangelism. It must be active in seeking out the lost and leading them to Christ.

The church is also to be a training ground for Christians. It should offer instruction in the Word of God and the Christian life. It should be a place where believers can grow in their faith and be equipped to serve Christ.

The church is to be a fellowship of believers, united in Christ and sharing His love with one another. It should be a place of love, encouragement, and support. We are to *bear one another's burdens* (Gal 6:2) and *exhort one another daily* (Heb 3:13).

The church is also to be a witnessing community, sharing the good news of Jesus Christ with those around us. We are to be *"the light of the world"* (Matt 5:14) and *"the salt of the earth"* (Matt 5:13). As we seek to revitalize our churches, let us keep these things in mind. Let us pray that God will help us see His church as he sees it and to be the people he intends for us to be.

Church revitalization starts by seeing what is around us.

Do you ever think of the people who once had a vision for Christ's work on that very spot where the church sits? At a point in time God spoke to someone's heart about planting a church. Probably through much prayer that person was reassured that God called him or her to start that church, so he or she set forth telling others of the plan. The person started looking for locations to meet. Some start in houses, others in a storefront, and others in borrowed churches. Then the day came when the location was found. An empty piece of property would become the home, the location where your church now sits. The ground was broken, construction started—and now stands your church.

Can you picture all the sacrifice and hard work that got them that far? Do you sense the passion that must have rung out through the building at one time? Can you imagine the celebration and enthusiasm that must have existed in that first service? Can you hear the testimonies of salvation and sanctification that must have been experienced here? Or do you see only neglect and abandonment? Do you see anything at all?

Are you a pastor or worker of an existing church that has fallen into disrepair? Do you have little to show for the sacrifices of your predecessors? Do your members simply walk through the building not really thinking about what used to exist here and what it could become again? Do they view their involvement as going up on Sunday morning, walking into church, sitting down and listening, then going home without ever having gone out of their way to make any change at all? Are there young people present who are only peripherally aware of what is happening around them?

If so, I encourage you today to think back on the history of this place. Think about those whose blood, sweat, and tears made this church possible. See if from their example you can catch a vision for what this place could be again. It will take hard work. It will take dedication. But if you are willing to put in the effort, I believe that God will bless your church and bring revival through your revitalization effort.

This is not an easy task I'm putting before you. But it is one I believe is worth undertaking. After all, what else are we called to do but to be the hands and feet of Christ in this world? And what better way to do that than by bringing new life into His body, the church? I encourage you today to begin the process of church revitalization by simply taking a look around you and seeing what could be again.

From the very first time that God called someone to serve Him and began His work on earth, he has been focused on people. He is constantly moving and working in order to save the lost and bring them into salvation through Christ. And he has never stopped doing this work throughout history. As Christians, it is our responsibility to continue His mission by being a part of it as well. We are called to be a part of church revitalization—reaching out to our communities and helping those around us grow closer to Christ.

It can often be difficult for us today to really see needs around us or understand the impact that we can have on those who are lost. This is especially true in our own churches. We can get so comfortable and complacent in our own routines that we fail to see how we can make a difference in the lives of others. But if we take the time to look around us, I believe that we will begin to see the many opportunities that exist for us to reach out and make a real difference. There are people all around us who are lost and in need of a Savior. And there are also people within our own churches who may be struggling or even close to giving up altogether. It is our responsibility as Christians to reach out to these people and help them find new life in Christ.

To do this effectively, it is important for us to have a vision for what we are trying to accomplish. We need to know what we are called to do and where we are going. This is why we must be in prayer and seeking God's guidance for our lives. We need to be asking Him to show us where we should focus our attention and what needs he wants us to meet. Only when we have a clear vision from God will we be able to effectively reach out and help those around us.

How do we see the church that we attend?

And what do you see when you drive by a boarded-up church? We become so familiar with our surroundings that we are blind to the community around us. Do you see a church that died because it was stuck in tradition or legalism? Do you become sad, knowing that it represents a light on a hill that has become darkened? When you pass a small church on the side of the street of a small town, do you see a vital part of the faith community providing a witness of the gospel? Or do you see a church that drains resources and should be closed so that the resources could be utilized better elsewhere? Small and rural churches are vital to the work of the kingdom. Over seven in ten churches have fewer than one hundred in attendance any given Sunday.

These small churches are the backbone of the faith community in America. They are places where people can come and experience the presence of God, receive spiritual guidance and encouragement, find a sense of community and fellowship, and be challenged to grow in their faith. For us to truly be effective in church revitalization, we need to have a heart for these small churches. We need to see them not as burdens or nuisances but as essential parts of the body of Christ. We need to be willing to invest our time, energy, and resources into helping them grow and thrive. Only then will we begin to see real transformation taking place in our communities. Some say that revitalizing churches is a waste of resources and the money can be spent on planting and replanting. I totally reject this notion. Although planting is a vital part of church revitalization it is not the only answer. Every church great and small are valuable in God's plan for reaching the community around us.

How do you see the community you live in?

Some see rural America as a place to retreat from the noise and the confusion of city life, to relax and enjoy recreation activities. Others see rural America as a decaying and dying landscape where people are stuck in the past and are as run-down as the old homes and churches that dot the landscape. Still others see rural people as closed-minded bigots who reject modern society and perpetrate longstanding racial and economic biases. We can become so familiar and comfortable with our surroundings that we become blind to the very community we live in.

What do you see? Christ sees people who are without a shepherd. To Him these communities represent individuals who have been devastated by the ravaging effects of sin and are in desperate need of the gospel. Too often when driving through the countryside of rural communities, we fail to see like this. We see only what our natural eyes allow us to see—the physical landscape and the structures that exist within it. But we don't see the hearts of the people who live there—their needs and their hurts, their fears and their struggles. We simply see a community that looks different than our own.

If we're going to be effective in church revitalization, then we need to learn to see rural America through the eyes of

Christ. Only then will we be able to truly understand the needs of these communities and how we can best reach them with the gospel. Only when this happens will true transformation begin taking place.

What can you as a pastor or church leader do to help change small and rural North American churches? Rural areas of this country are simply not prepared for the challenges that come with modern society. The loss of manufacturing jobs and the closing of businesses have left many communities without an economic foundation on which to build their future. As people flock to cities for work, rural areas are often left struggling just to stay alive. And when Christian leaders fail to see these realities and act on them, then we will never be able to effectively reach people in these communities with the gospel.

When the apostle Paul took the gospel into other lands during his lifetime, he did so by recognizing ways in which they were like ancient Israel. He saw similarities between their cultures and customs. He saw the social structures that existed, such as government and commerce. And he applied these lessons to his ministry of planting churches that would change their society for Christ.

When we enter into rural America, we must do so with a similar mindset. We must see the people in these communities as having needs similar to those who lived centuries ago—even though they may be very different in many ways! If you're not familiar with what's going on in rural America today, then it will be impossible for you to address their needs and connect them with the gospel message. You need to learn about the history of your area: how it was settled, why certain industries were established there, how agriculture played a major role, and how all these things have shaped the people who live there.

Once we begin to see rural America through the eyes of Christ, then we can begin to address their needs with practical strategies for church revitalization. We need to create new ministries that cater specifically to the unique challenges facing these people, such as job training or addiction recovery programs. We need to connect them with neighboring churches that are interested in engaging in outreach activities together. And we need to teach them about God's love for them and His desire for transformation in their lives and communities. Only when we step out in faith and truly seek change for our communities will true revitalization take place—both in individual hearts as well as within our society at large.

Small churches must see and believe that they have the capacity to be everything God desires them to be.

Although the small congregation is only a fraction of the size of a megachurch, it may be quite sizable in terms of its members and influence. Small congregations have the ability to be vibrant participants in God's mission on earth. We want to do better. We can do better. We *will* do better. But we can't do it alone. Small and rural churches need to see that they are not the forgotten stepchildren. They are not secondary to the body of Christ. They are not just some afterthought of denominational leaders. Even though their physical size would indicate otherwise, they are not less important for kingdom work in the community where they reside due to their stature. They are the essential elements of the body God designed for a specific purpose. They have been given keys to unlocking blessing and restoration in their communities because they are present there.

Small and rural churches must be courageous as they seek change in order to remain sustainable, relevant, and impacting in their areas. It is imperative that small churches work together (along with other agencies or church bodies) if they truly want to make positive changes for future generations. The goal will not be easy, but the outcome is worth the effort! Revitalization does not happen overnight; it requires diligence from us all each day. Change never happens by accident. It takes intentional action on our part coupled with faithfulness and persistence. We should know this well enough to be motivated to move forward.

For small and rural churches to truly thrive, they must embrace change and go after new opportunities that can help them grow and revitalize. They should see themselves as the vital DNA of their communities and recognize the important role they have in transforming those around them with God's love and grace. We all have a part to play in this work, so let us commit ourselves fully to it, knowing that we are bringing about real, transformative change! With hard work, courage, determination, and persistence on our part—along with faith in God's power at work within us—small churches will continue to thrive for generations to come!

Small congregations must first see their purpose with God's eyes.

Small and rural churches play an important role in the kingdom. You don't see megachurches on country roads thirty minutes or more from the interstate. You don't see lots of outreach money pouring into sparsely populated counties. God has a specific purpose and plan for each small rural church that is dotted across this vast country we live in. If you would count the number of people who attend megachurches versus the number attending the countless quantities of small churches, you would clearly see that the majority attend these small and rural churches.

There is power in the small number of people of your church. The big churches can't do in your community what you can do, and that's through the power of your presence. Your presence and your boots on the ground make all the difference. But for that power and presence to happen, you must recognize and decide to get out into the community and build those relationships. That's the purpose you have, to make relationships. We were created by God, for God, in the image of God to have a relationship with Him first, but also to have relationships with each other. That's the purpose God has for you.

With that purpose in mind, you'll find the courage to do the hard work of revitalization. You must commit yourself fully to this mission, knowing that together we can create real and transformative change in our communities! If you're a pastor or leader of a small and rural church, don't be discouraged by your size or location. Embrace your mission and purpose as a vital part of God's plan for transforming the world around you. With faith, courage, persistence, and determination on your side, nothing can stop you from bringing about positive change in your community!

Billy Graham said, "The greatest need in the world today is for revival in the rural churches." I believe that is still true today. Small and rural churches have a big impact on their communities, and we need them to be strong and thriving! We all have a role to play in revitalizing these churches, so let us commit ourselves fully to the task at hand. With God's help, we can make a difference!

Actions speak more loudly than words, and it's time for small and rural churches to take some bold steps forward to continue being relevant and impactful in their communities. It won't be easy, but it's worth it! Let us commit ourselves to this work, knowing that we are bringing about real and transformative change!

Small churches must be unashamed in their obedience.

Many churches require rejuvenation because their people have ceased to be obedient to the Lord in every aspect of their lives. That seems like a harsh and rude statement, but it's the truth. Sloth has crept into the church's life, and as a consequence, the church has turned its attention to itself. It has become less and less concerned with those the outside the walls. We must acknowledge the necessity for obedience, even if it kills us, to experience actual revitalization. Obedience is the only true indicator of devotion to God and complete dedication to His work.

When we are not obedient, it shows that we really do not fear God. It is only through obedience that we can hope to have any type of relationship with Him. If we want our churches to be revitalized, then we must start with obedience to God's commands. This means that every single member of the church must be on board with this change. It will not happen overnight, but if we are patient and persistent, true change will come about!

The small church has a unique opportunity to lead the way in terms of church revitalization. We have the chance to be nimble and adaptable, unlike our larger counterparts. We can be pioneers in this work, and we can show the world what it looks like for a church to be truly dedicated to obedience.

Acknowledging that we have been disobedient is the first step to seeing as God sees. This may be a difficult thing to do, but it is essential if we want to move forward. We must admit our mistakes and our sinfulness and ask for forgiveness. Only then can we hope to be forgiven and to have a fresh start.

What does God see when he looks at your church? God sees a body of believers who have all the potential within them that he has deposited in you. He knows the plans he has for you (Jer 29:11). The promise that God made was not to just one person but to the children of Israel. The church has the same promise from the Father. He knows what he wants for each congregation to achieve and accomplish in the community they are in. We just have to see as God sees us. I encourage you today to begin the process of church revitalization by simply taking a look around you and seeing what could be. Pray for God to reveal needs around you and then take steps of faith to reach out and meet those needs.

Chapter 6

Repent: Mistaken Identity and Lost Purpose

If My people who are called by My name will humble themselves, and pray and seek My face, and turn from their wicked ways, then I will hear from heaven, and will forgive their sin and heal their land.

—2 CHR 7:14

AN INCORRECT VIEW OF the church is detrimental to the effectiveness of the congregation. We must understand that the way we observe the church can affect our effectiveness in ministry. To revitalize and repent, we must recognize that the church is not synonymous with man-made institutions. Rather, the church is a universal body through which God has called us to work together in His name. By understanding the church's identity, we can start down the path of revival and redemption. With repentance as our guide, we will be able to tap into the purpose and potential of God's church, discovering new life and vitality for ourselves and our communities. So if you feel your church is dying or stuck in a rut, remember to heed the call to repent and discover a renewed sense of purpose in God's holy temple.

Understanding the identity of the church can change the way we think about our purpose and potential. We are no longer limited by our limitations. Instead, we are called to work together to advance the kingdom of God. However, before we can truly tap into the power of the church, we must first repent of our mistaken views. We must recognize that the way we have been observing the church is damaging to its effectiveness. Only then can we begin to move down the path of revival and redemption.

Small and rural churches often point out their inadequacies or devalue their effectiveness in light of their numbers. Understand that small and rural churches have as much value and worth as any other congregation. As long as they remain committed to the church's true identity and purpose, they can continue being a vital part of God's kingdom. Let us all seek the path of repentance so that we can rediscover what it means to truly serve our Lord and Savior. And may our churches flourish in love, joy, and peace for His glory.

Repentance is needed for churches with self-esteem that is negative and self-defeating. The need is to turn their thinking from incorrect views of the church to boldness and courage that is the call of God to His people. With a renewed sense of purpose, church leaders can revitalize their churches and open the doors to greater growth and vitality. Let us all be willing and ready to turn from the mistakes of our past so that we can live boldly for Christ and join together in His kingdom work. May we all find new life as we seek repentance and discover the richness of church life that God has set before us.

When we church members have a low opinion of ourselves, it's hard to imagine that our church could be anything other than it is. But when we repent and turn to God, he can change our church and use it for His glory. When we see the church through His eyes, we'll find new life and purpose in being part of His church. So let us all repent and see our church through the eyes of God so that we can be part of His plan to change the world.

A church in decline finds it easy to see all that's wrong and lose hope for the future. But when we repent and turn to God, he can breathe new life into our church and move us forward once again. With a new sense of purpose, we can discover the richness and joy of church life that God has in store for us. Let us all muster the courage to face our challenges with humility, love, and faith so that we can join together in God's work and serve Him with all our hearts.

Your church may be feeling adrift or in need of a reboot. The long-term goal is to acquire the trust and confidence of your congregation. So don't give up hope if your church isn't thriving. Remind yourself that God may use even a church in repentance and rebirth for His glory. God delights in using the common to demonstrate the uncommon.

When we come to Christ, we are given a new identity. We are no longer defined by our past mistakes or failures but rather by our new relationship with Christ. This new identity can be the foundation for a fresh start in your church. If your church has lost its way, seek forgiveness and turn back to God. He will give you the wisdom and strength you need to lead your church into a bright future. Jesus had John pen a letter to the Ephesus church to do this very thing. To remember and to repent.

Repentance is not easy, but it's well worth it. When we turn from our sin and back to God, we find new life and purpose. We also find hope for the future. So if your church is struggling, don't give up hope. You can take your church from a dreary present to a bright future brimming with hope and optimism if you have humility and bravery.

The church is the bride of Christ, and our identity should reflect that. If we humble ourselves and ask for His aid, he will lead us to a new life and a fresh sense of purpose. Let us be empowered by love, joy, and faith as we assume our duties as church members and leaders. And let us never forget that through Christ we are new creations.

The definition of *identity* is "the distinguishing character or personality of an individual." In this case, the identity of the church should represent Christ as His bride. We are people with a new purpose. We are Christians, called by God to be a light in the darkness and hope for the hopeless. Just the way that Jesus was the embodiment of the Father himself, we as the church, should be the image and character of Jesus Christ to a lost world that does not know Him.

Revitalization comes through repenting of mistaken identity and lost purpose.

Word association exercises are often good indicators of the mindset and worldview of the participants involved. Sociologists often use this method to determine the thought process of their subjects. If you ask a group of people to express words that they would associate with *small,* you will get a wide range of responses. Most, if not all, of the responses, are negatively charged in the application. This should be of no surprise since the word *small* in the dictionary has been portrayed negatively in many of the same ways, such as "having a comparatively little size or slight dimensions"; "minor in influence, power, or rank"; "little or close to zero in an objectively measurable aspect." With the latter definition mentioned, it is no wonder that the small church struggles with the loss of identity and loss of purpose for themselves.

If you would do the same exercise with the term *small church,* you would get many of the same negative results: "insignificant numbers," "lack of money," and "a handful of inexperienced and entry-level pastors." Often people inside and outside the church define small churches by the numbers they have or even the lack. Numbers are most often used when judging the small church, pointing out its inadequacies or devaluing its effectiveness.

Why do small churches suffer from mistaken identity? Because they see their small sizes as a problem. They are quick to compare themselves to the megachurch down the street and feel that they're coming up short. They see their lack of resources and manpower and feel that they can't compete. As a result, they lose sight of their purpose. They forget that God has called them to be a light in their community, not to compete with other churches. They forget that they are to be salt and not sugar. They become focused on their insecurities and shortcomings instead of the great commission.

The answer for the small church is not to try to become something it's not. The answer is to embrace its smallness and use it to advantage, to be the church that's intimate and personal, that knows its members by name, that's focused on discipleship, not numbers, and is salt and light in a dark world. If the small church can do this, it will not only survive but thrive as well. It will find its identity and purpose in Christ. And it will be a witness to the world to the fact that it's still possible to be the church despite all the odds.

Is our church identified by numbers and/or size?

"Esteem has to do with identity and well-being; it is connected with the discovery or recovery of one's God-given individuality." When we lose our sense of identity, we also lose our sense of purpose. We may go through life feeling aimless and unfulfilled, not knowing who we are or why we're here. This can happen when we forget our identity as children of God. We were created in His image, and he has a specific plan and purpose for our lives. When we live according to His will, we find true fulfillment. But when we try to be someone we're not, or we chase after things that don't matter, we end up empty and disappointed. We may have all the "things" we thought would make us happy, but they won't satisfy us if we're not living in God's will. Don't waste your life chasing after things that won't satisfy you. Seek God's will for your life and you'll find true identity and real purpose.

This is the struggle for the churches with such dynamics within its body. They see themselves as insignificant and many times impotent. Their self-esteem is negative and self-defeating. Psychologist Marsha Sinetar has this to say about the subject: "Self-esteem is just an idea we have about ourselves . . . about our competence, our worth, and our power . . . a picture we have in our minds about ourselves." She further suggests, "We often lose sight of our identity and self-esteem, or find it distorted, damaged, or hidden."

The enemy's tactic is to keep the church so busy with "good works" that it never has time to search its own heart and discover its identity in Christ. It is a strategy of identity theft, and it robs the church of its power and purpose. When the church loses sight of its identity, it becomes like a ship without a rudder, tossed to and fro by every wind of doctrine. The apostle Paul warned Timothy about this very thing: *The time will come when they will not endure sound doctrine, but according to their own desires,* because *they have itching ears, they will heap up for themselves teachers; and they will turn* their *ears away from the truth, and be turned aside to fables* (2 Tim 4:3–4).

The church today is in grave danger of following the same pattern. We have allowed our identity to be hijacked by the world, and as a result we are losing our way. We have exchanged the truth of God for a lie, and we are reaping the consequences. It is time for the church to wake up and take back what belongs to us—our identity in Christ. We must claim our rightful place as children of God, joint heirs with Christ, and co-laborers with him in his work. It is time for us to walk in the power and purpose that is ours in Christ.

It is not the size of the church that determines its effectiveness. It is not the number of programs that makes it significant. It is not the amount in the treasury that determines its influence. It is not how many members sit in the pews each Sunday morning that establishes its purpose. The church finds its identity by understanding *whose it is.* When it knows whose it is, it will know why it exists. When the church understands its purpose, it will have all the power it needs to fulfill its destiny. When the church understands that it belongs to God and exists for His purposes, it will have all the power and influence it needs to be effective in the world.

Does my view of the identity of the church match that of Christ?

The mission is to rediscover and capture that healthy God-given image that he intended and to recover the small church's self-esteem and be transformed in it. Sinetar concludes, "[Self-esteem is feelings] and self-pictures that we make real, and only we can change it for the better, for our good, forever." It is no secret that the church today is facing an identity crisis. In a world that is constantly changing and evolving, it can be difficult to know who we are and whose we are. This crisis of identity has led to a loss of purpose and a feeling of insignificance among many Christians. But the good news is that this doesn't have to be the case. Christ Himself is our identity, and he has called us to a specific purpose: to love Him and others. When we rediscover our identity in Christ, we will be able to live out our God-given purpose with confidence and joy.

When identity is lost or distorted, then purpose is lost or distorted as well. The uncertainty of self-causes purpose to drift from the center, and left unchecked and uncorrected, it will lead to areas never intended to be dwelled in. No church happens accidentally. Intention and purpose are driving the new congregation of believers. For far too long the small church has bought a bill of goods that does not have to be true. They have bought into the assumption that since they are small then they must be insignificant. *Small* does not have to mean be negative but in fact, it is positive. The words that can accentuate the positive can be *close, community, family, intimacy,* and *trusting,* but full potential is another.

If you take a moment and think about the size of the church, then you can see that the small church has tremendous potential to do the mighty things for God. The smallest obedient deed can be magnified because no one expects much from them. God receives multiplied glory amid His small body of believers. The light is the brightest in the deepest darkness. Even so is God amidst His chosen few.

The small church has often been misinterpreted. His people have often fallen into the trap of believing that because they are little, they must be unimportant. Small does not have to imply negative in any way; rather, it may be beneficial. Close, community, family, intimacy, and trust are a few of the ways to enhance the good qualities.

The small church often loses sight of its potential and purpose, becoming bogged down in the day-to-day tasks and forgetting why it exists—which, of course, is to glorify God and advance His kingdom, not its own. When the small church remembers its purpose, it can change the world.

Is the church fulfilling its ordained purpose for God?

The church was never meant to be a country club for the religious elite. It was ordained by God to be a light in the darkness, hope for the hopeless, and a city on a hill that cannot be hidden (Matt 5:14–16). But somewhere along the way we lost sight of our purpose. We became comfortable in our little Christian bubbles, forgetting that there are still people out there who desperately need to hear the good news of the gospel. We turned inward instead of reaching outward. And in doing so, we lost our way. It's time for the church to wake up, repent, and remember who we are. We're not a social club or a self-help group. We're the body of Christ, called to spread His love and light to a lost and dying world (Matt 28:19–20). It's time for us to start living like it.

Here are some encouraging things to do if you're not sure where to begin:

1. **Pray for your community.** Ask God to show you where there are needs that the church can meet. Pray that God will open the eyes of your church leaders to see where they can make a difference. The body of Christ has been given a mission by God Himself—we are to spread the gospel and make disciples of all nations. But are we doing that? Are we living out our purpose? Many churches today have lost sight of their mission. They've become comfortable and complacent. They've allowed themselves to be drawn away from the Great Commission by other pursuits. Prayer is the logical place to start. Can you imagine what could happen if the church had their eyes opened and started treating people the way Jesus treated them, with compassion and pure love for their souls.

2. **Step outside your comfort zone.** Talk to people who don't look like you, think like you, or believe what you believe. Listen more than you talk. You might be surprised by what you learn. The church has always been meant to be a safe place for sinners to come and find forgiveness and new life in Jesus.

   Sadly, too often the church today is more interested in maintaining its power and influence than it is in fulfilling its God-given mission. We have become comfortable in our little worlds and lost sight of the fact that there are people all around us who are hurting, lost, and in need of a Savior. It's time for the church to take a good look at itself and rediscover its goal. It's time for Christians to start reaching out to the lost and the broken and sharing the good news of Jesus Christ. It's past time for us to be the church that God intended us to be. Allowing ourselves to be in places that are uncomfortable. It may be volunteering in a shelter or addiction center. Possibly it could be a jail ministry or helping at a center for abused women. Regardless of what it is it must be where hurting and broken people are.

3. **Serve your community.** Find a local soup kitchen or homeless shelter and offer to help out. Or start a food drive for a local food bank or start a food pantry in your church. Show your neighbors that you care about them and are willing to help meet their needs. The church's purpose is to serve God by serving others.

4. **Be the light.** When you see someone being treated poorly, speak up. Show that person kindness and respect, even if he or she doesn't deserve it. You never know when your act of kindness will change someone's life. The world is full of broken and hurting people. They're lost, they're searching, and they're looking for meaning in their lives. As Christians we have the light of Christ to offer them. But too often we keep that light hidden under a bushel. We're afraid to speak up, to reach out, to show Christ's love concretely. What if we were the ones who made the difference in some people's

lives? What if our acts of kindness and compassion led them to Christ? Let's be the light of Christ to a world that's lost and searching. Let's show them His love, His compassion, and His mercy. It could change their lives and ours—forever.

5. **Invite people in.** You don't have to be perfect to invite someone to church. And it's often the imperfect people who need Christ the most. So don't be afraid to extend a hand of friendship, even if you're not sure where they stand spiritually. The church is a place where broken people can come to find healing and hope. But somewhere along the way we've lost sight of that. We've become more concerned with keeping out the "undesirables" than we are with welcoming the lost and hurting.

We possess the greatest message ever told. Why not share it? The good news is that it's never too late to change. We can start today by reaching out to those who are searching for something more. Let's be the church that Christ intended us to be—a place of hope, healing, and love. If not, it's time for a change. It's time to get back to the basics. It's time to start acting like the church again. The world is lost and dying, but there is hope. The church has the answer, but we must be willing to step out of our comfort zones and share it. Let's remember who we are and why we're here. We're the body of Christ, called to love and serve a lost and dying world. Let's start living like it.

Identity Abuse

Each one of us is unique in his or her own certain ways and the church is no different. A church is unique in the fact that it's set in a particular place geographically, and it must interact with its community in a social context that is unique to them alone. Ultimately our identity comes from the head of the church, Jesus Christ. That identity is expressed in and through the people and places where they exist. Our job is to pour life and encouragement and truth into the community in which we live. In doing so, the church's identity is nurtured and we learn to express ourselves well and look forward to life and relationships within that context.

Unfortunately, this is not always the case. Time and environment in the community changes, and when the community no longer sees the church as a viable and relevant piece of the society, then the identity of the church is abused and disrupted. Attendance starts declining. Families move away and other families do not replace them. The way the church perceives itself changes. The church will start to believe the lies from the enemy that they are small, they are insignificant, they are no longer relevant, and they are not adequate. This can have a dramatic effect on the congregation and the purpose and effectiveness of the church as it begins seeing itself as unable to accomplish the work that God had laid out before it previously, which in turn begins negatively affecting its presence in the community.

The church needs to get back to the basics of who they are in Christ. It starts with repentance and a recommitment to living out the truth of who we are in Christ. We need to return to our first love, Jesus Christ, and let Him renew our minds and change our perspectives. Only then can we hope to correct the lies that we have been believing about ourselves and see ourselves the way God sees us, which is as people who are fearfully and wonderfully made (Ps 139:14). We are His children, chosen and predestined for good work (Eph 1:4–5), loved by Him with an everlasting love (Jer 31:3), and accepted in the Beloved (Eph 1:6). These truths about our identity in Christ should radically change the way we see ourselves and live our lives. It is when we see ourselves correctly, through the lens of Scripture, that we can start accomplishing the work God has called us to do.

We need to be careful, though, because sometimes to get back to our roots and Christian values we can start relying on our own strength and understanding. We should be careful that we don't become legalistic in our approach or try going back to a time that is no longer relevant. We need to contextualize the gospel for the community. We the church can get caught up in trying to do the work of God and then lose sight of who we are in Christ. Our identity is found in Christ alone and not in our works.

The enemy will try to deceive us and tell us lies about who we are, but we need to stand firm on the truth of who we are in Christ. We are His beloved children, chosen for good works, and loved with an everlasting love. These truths should shape and change the way we see ourselves and the way we live our lives. Let us return to our first love, Jesus Christ, and allow Him renew our minds and change our perspectives. Only then can we hope reject the lies that we have been believing about ourselves and see ourselves the way God sees us, which is fearfully and wonderfully made.

Elaine Briefman, a licensed marriage and Christian counselor, and owner of Fishing4Truth Ministries, writes,

> The enemy of our soul is constantly seeking to destroy our identity in Christ. He does this by lying to us, telling us things that are not true about ourselves. These lies can be so convincing that, after years of constant bombardment, we begin to believe them and act as if they are true. The enemy will tell you that you're not good enough, smart enough, or talented enough. He will tell you that you're not worthy of love or respect. He will tell you that you're a failure and that you will never amount to anything. But the truth is that none of these things are true. You *are* good enough, smart enough, and talented enough. You *are* worthy of love and respect. And you *can* succeed in life.[1]

The only way to combat these lies is to know the truth about yourself. And the truth is that you are a child of God, created in His image and likeness. You are fearfully and wonderfully made. You are redeemed and forgiven. You are loved and accepted. You are significant and valuable. You have a purpose and a destiny. You are defined not by your past but by your future in Christ. So don't let the enemy steal your identity. Don't let him tell you who you are. Instead, let God define you. Let *Him* tell you who you are. And then live your life in a way that reflects His truth.

1. Briefman, *Jesus Is In*, 224–25.

The same crisis is true for the congregations of churches that have struggled for years and decades with the lie of inadequacy and insufficiency. Billy Graham said, "The greatest need in the world today is for people to know God and to understand His love for them." When we understand and return to God, we begin understanding His love for us. And when we understand His love for us, we can't help but share it with others.

Pastor Briefman goes on to say, many Christians (and churches) "are unaware of how much their motivation and confidence have been damaged by the ploys of the enemy. Often Christians will unknowingly accept lies as truth and it damages their identity. Once your identity is strengthened and healed, your ability to live in the fullness of what God intended becomes completely possible."[2]

If you've been struggling with a lost sense of identity or purpose, it's time to repent and return to the truth. You are loved and accepted by God. You have a purpose and destiny. And you can live a life that reflects His truth.

We must allow God to heal our identity so that we can fulfill our purpose that he has for us in our community and our world.

2. "Things We Conquer" in Briefman, "Invite Pastor Elaine."

Chapter 7

Respond: The Role of Prayer in Revitalization

With what shall I come before the Lord, and bow my-self before the High God? Shall I come before Him with burnt offerings, with calves a year old? Will the Lord be pleased with thousands of rams, ten thousand rivers of oil? Shall I give my firstborn for my transgression, the fruit of my body for the sin of my soul? He has shown you, O man, what is good; and what does the Lord require of you but to do justly, to love mercy, and to walk humbly with your God?

—Mic 6:6–8

What is potential? It is your unused strengths, hidden talents, untapped abilities, and capped or locked-up capabilities. There is a great wealth of potential within you. Potential can be characterized by a stick of dynamite, which is an object that has great capabilities bound inside it, capabilities of great destruction or construction depending on the use. All that potential and power can be released by a single spark. You must decide if you will deprive or bless the world with those gifts that are locked away inside you. If you decide you do want to have that potential released, then the next step is to understand the principles God has established for unlocking that potential.

Potential is released through intentional and purposeful prayer. If we are to see our communities revitalized, we must begin with prayer, through which we access the power of God to break through the barriers that stand in our way. We must cry out to God for His intervention and ask Him to move in our midst. Only then will we see true change take place. Prayer is not a magic formula, but it is the key that unlocks the door to all that God has for us. Let us begin by calling on the name of the Lord and see what he will do!

Everything starts with prayer

Simply stated, prayer is talking with God. We pray when we open our hearts to the Almighty. As simple as this is, it is also something people need to hear. Too many people feel that prayer is certain words spoken *very* loudly. Others feel prayer is something that takes place in a particular place or with a special posture. But none of these are requirements for true prayer. In fact, you can sound holy and not be doing anything other than talking to yourself or the ceiling. True prayer is open, honest, humble, and personal. It is a matter of relationship, and it can happen no other way.

Create a culture or lifestyle of prayer

Conversation is a part of any vital and growing relationship. We sometimes measure the quality of a marriage relationship by how well the couple communicates. To state it another way, one of the first things people point to as evidence that a marriage is in trouble is a lack of communication. If you do not have a desire to communicate, then you do not have a desire for a meaningful relationship.

The same is true for our relationship with the Father. A true, honest, heartfelt conversation is a sign of a healthy relationship. A lack of conversation, or conversation only in public, is a sign of a relationship in trouble. It is through the prayer life of a committed, devoted servant that God can bring out the strength and power he wants to demonstrate in the child of God.

The role of prayer in our lives, then, is simply to help us grow closer to God. It is the key that unlocks the door to all he has for us. When we come before Him with open hearts and minds, he can begin working in us and through us to accomplish great things. We must never forget that it all starts with prayer. It is through prayer that we communicate with Him and build a deeper relationship with Him.

Prayer is also a key part of seeing our communities revitalized. As we pray for God to move in our midst, we will see true change take place. Prayer is vital to our relationship with God. Prayer is the means in which we will start seeing people around us the way God sees them. We will start to see them as lost souls worth being saved and experiencing the glory of God in their lives.

Listening is part of prayer

Paul commands us to pray always when he writes, *Pray without ceasing* (1 Thess 5:17). It cannot mean we are to be in a head-bowed, eyes-closed posture all day long. Paul is not referring to non-stop talking but rather an attitude of God-consciousness and God-surrender that we carry with us all the time. Every waking moment is to be lived in an awareness that God is with us and that he is actively involved and engaged in our thoughts and actions. The Greek reads, *Pray without intermission,* without allowing prayerless gaps to intervene between the times of prayer. When we are in a state of continual, conscious prayer, we can then hear God respond and speak to us so we can know and hear His heart. If prayer is to be a conversation with the Almighty, then we must allow time for God to speak to us. Otherwise, we're simply giving a lecture to God, informing Him of everything that we've already decided needs to be done, and then prayer is more information *for* God rather than guidance *from* God. What God says to you is far more important than what you say to God.

Prayer is not a monologue but rather a conversation. It is an opportunity for us to hear from God. To do this, we must be still and quiet before Him, allowing Him to speak to our hearts. We can then take His guidance and use it to see our communities revitalized.

Repentance is essential for effective prayer

Prayer changes us. Prayer doesn't change God, it doesn't change things, nor does it always change circumstances. Prayer changes *us*. Our prayers often reflect the truth that everyone thinks of changing humanity—but no one thinks of changing himself or herself. Real prayer changes us. Repentance is the turning from our ways to God's ways.

Real prayer is not only soul-satisfying; it is life-changing. When you and I spend time with Jesus, he changes us. To pray is to change. Prayer is the central avenue God uses to transform us. If we're unwilling to change, we abandon prayer as a noticeable characteristic of our lives. The closer we come to the heartbeat of God, the more we see our own needs, and the more we desire to be conformed to Christ. The transformation that Christ provides is more of a "turn-formation," turning from our evil ways. Don't pray unless you want to change. Prayer propels us into action. Prayer advances God's kingdom. Prayer ignites a church to move outside its walls.

When the church prays, things happen!

If we are to see our communities revitalized, we must be willing to change ourselves. Repentance is essential for effective prayer. As we turn from our ways to God's ways, we will see true transformation take place.

Obeying the voice that comes through prayer

Prayer unleashes the power of God. Two characteristics dominated the apostles' prayer meetings: God's presence and God's power. Is it any wonder that the evil one seeks valiantly to keep Christ-followers from praying? When we don't pray, Satan has won the battle. But when we *do* pray, the presence and the power of God are unleashed. The disciples in Jerusalem experienced the power of God in a very tangible and real way. *When they had prayed, the place where they were assembled together was shaken* (Acts 4:31). We're also told that the power of the Lord was present to heal them.

The ministry of Jesus Christ was characterized by prayer. So must ours be as well if we are to see our communities revitalized. As we pray, we will experience the presence and power of God like never before. We must be willing to change ourselves, obeying the voice that comes through prayer. Only then will we see true transformation take place.

What is the role of prayer in revitalization?

In 2 Chr 7:14 the Lord says, *"If My people who are called by My name will humble themselves, and pray and seek My face, and turn from their wicked ways, then I will hear from heaven, and will forgive their sin and heal their land."*

Very few of the eight billion people on this planet will ever maximize the full potential that God has placed inside them. Most people live mediocre lives. The full extent of their capabilities and talents goes untapped. They are not even aware of the tremendous potential they possess.

Maximizing your potential requires effort. It is not something that will happen by accident. You must be intentional about it. You must decide that you are going to live a life of excellence and not mediocrity. You must be willing to do the hard work necessary to tap into your potential. But it will be worth it! When you reach your full potential, you will be able to accomplish great things for God's glory. You will be a blessing to others and a testimony of His goodness.

One way that you can maximize your potential is by prayer, which is one of the most powerful tools God has given us, a way for us to connect with Him and tap into His power. When we pray, we are tapping into the very power of almighty God! When we pray, we are releasing our faith and believe that God can do anything. We are declaring His sovereignty and authority over our lives. We are asking Him to do the impossible.

Potential can be said to be explosive energy. I believe God has placed an explosive power in you that can raise the dead, and that power is the Holy Spirit Himself. God wants you to be everything he has intended for you to be since before time began. When you reach your full potential in Christ, you will be an unstoppable force for the gospel. You will see people set free from every bond and slavery. You will see the sick healed, the blind receive their sight, and the dead raised to life!

Prayer is essential if we are going to see our communities transformed. We must be willing to change ourselves, obeying the voice that comes through prayer. Only then will we see true transformation take place.

If you are interested in seeing your community revitalized, I encourage you to start praying. Pray for God to break through the strongholds that are holding people back. Pray for His power to be released in your community. Pray for revival!

God has a pattern for which he responds to our prayers. When we pray and seek Him with humility, he hears us. When we turn from our wicked ways, he forgives us. And when we ask, he heals our land. If you're ready to see your community healed, start by praying according to 2 Chr 7:14. Then watch as God moves in power!

God desires that His people look to Him for all their needs, including revitalization. He is the only one who can bring true and lasting change. Will you commit to prayer for your community today?

We must ask ourselves these revealing questions: Is prayer the priority that propels our work for God? Do we have more faith in our plans or in God's promises? Answered prayer is the greatest evidence of God's power. Seeing God do the impossible in our lives or in the world around us gives us hope and courage to keep going. It reminds us that he is in control and that His plans are always best.

Maybe you're feeling that your prayers don't make a difference, that you've been praying for the same thing for years with no answer in sight. I want to encourage you to keep going! Don't give up! God is faithful and he will answer your prayers in His perfect timing.

We must remain humble and obedient to the voice of God if we want to see true transformation take place. Will you commit to prayer for your church and community today? Again, I encourage you to start praying according to 2 Chr 7:14. Then watch as God moves!

Do we create an atmosphere of prayer as our church's lifestyle? Is your church known as a place that places high emphasis on prayer? Do you believe that God can do the impossible? If we want to see our churches and communities experience true transformation, then prayer must become a priority.

A lifestyle of prayer means that prayer is part of all aspects of the church. It's not just something we do on Sundays or Wednesdays. It's a 24/7, 365-days-a-year commitment. When we make prayer a priority, we're saying that we want God's will to be done in our lives and our world.

Do you take the time to hear God's voice in every area of your church? This means that you hear God speak in all areas of ministry, from the Sunday School curriculum to the financial decisions of the church. It also means that you hear God speak to you as an individual in every area of your life. Taking the time to hear God's voice changes everything. We begin seeing things the way he does and making decisions based on His will instead of our own. God is the only one who can bring true and lasting change. Will you commit to listening to His voice today?

Do we recognize and repent of attitudes and motives not reflective of God? This is a difficult thing to do, but it is so important. We must take a good, honest look at ourselves and ask God to reveal anything in our hearts that is not pleasing to Him. Once we have done that, we must be willing to repent and make things right. Only then can we move forward in obedience. If you're interested in seeing revival in your community, start by examining your own heart. Repent of anything that's not pleasing to God and make things right. Then commit to obeying His voice. When we're obedient to God, he will move in power and bring about lasting change.

Are we willing to be used by God even if it means stepping out of our comfort zones? This is a difficult thing to do, but it's so important. When we're willing to step out in faith and obey God, even when it's scary or difficult, he will use us to accomplish great things.

Revitalization efforts in any church can be started with all the right intentions, but it will fail every time if the revitalization effort is not bathed and covered in prayer to the Father desiring to accomplish His will for the congregation and community.

Prayer is a declaration of dependence

Prayer is also a declaration of dependence. When we pray, we are declaring that we are not self-sufficient and that we need God's help. We are admitting that we can't do it on our own and that we need His strength and guidance. This is a hard thing for us to do because we like to think of ourselves as independent and self-sufficient. We don't like to admit that we need help. But the truth is, we can't do it on our own. We need God's help every step of the way. Prayer is a humble acknowledgment of our dependence on God. It is admitting that we are weak and that we need His strength. And when we pray, we are also asking God to help us change. We are asking Him to transform us into the people he wants us to be.

Prayer is a powerful weapon

Prayer is a powerful weapon that we have at our disposal. It is one of the most effective ways we can fight against the enemy. When we pray, we're asking God to intervene on our behalf and to protect us from the enemy's schemes. The enemy is always looking for ways to destroy us. He wants to steal our joy, derail our plans, and ruin our relationships. But when we pray, we're putting up a shield of protection against his attacks. We're asking God to fight for us and to help us stay on the path he has laid out for us.

Prayer is also a way of declaring war against the enemy. When we pray, we're taking a stand against him and everything he stands for. We are saying that we will not back down or give in to his schemes. We're declaring that we're going to stand firm and fight for what is right.

Prayer is a vital part of the Christian life. It is how we connect with God and build our relationship with Him. It is how we declare our dependence on Him and ask for His help. It is how we fight against the enemy and stand firm in our faith. If we want to see God's power at work in our lives, then we need to be committed to prayer.

When we're in a state of continual, conscious prayer, we can then hear God respond and speak to us so that we can know and hear His heart. *Be still, and know that I am God; I will be exalted among the nations, I will be exalted in the earth!* (Ps 46:10). This verse is a reminder for us to be still and know that God is in control. We need to trust that he has a plan and that he knows what he is doing. We need to surrender our will to His and trust that he will lead us in the right direction. When we are still and quiet, we are better able to hear His voice. And when we follow His lead, we can be confident that he will exalt us and use us for His purposes.

Prayer is an essential part of the Christian life. It is how we connect with God and build our relationship with Him. If we want to see God's power at work in our lives, then we need to be committed to prayer. When we pray, we are declaring our dependence on God and asking for His help. We are also taking a stand against the enemy and declaring war against him. Prayer is a powerful weapon that we have at our disposal, and we need to use it if we want to see God's power at work in our lives.

Obeying the voice that comes through prayer

Undergirding all effective prayer is obedience. Just as a house cannot stand without a foundation, our prayers will not be effective if we are not obedient to the voice that comes through prayer. When we are disobedient, it's like trying to build a house on sand; it will not stand. But when we are obedient, it's like building a house on a rock; it will be strong and withstand the storms of life.

Obedience is essential to effective prayer because it is through obedience that we align our will with God's will. And when our will is aligned with God's will, we are in a position to receive all he has for us. We are also in a position to impact the world around us for His glory.

Ronald Reagan said, "Prayer is not a self-centered act; it is an expression of our total dependence on God." The obedience of prayer in a believer's life is an incredible, virtually untapped power source that is at our disposal. It is a supernatural act that God has called us to do that releases His presence and power into our lives to produce change. When we are obedient to the voice that comes through prayer, we can see God's power at work in our lives like never before.

When they had prayed, the place where they were assembled was shaken (Acts 4:31). Prayer is a spiritual act that can shake things up. It is not a passive act but one that releases the power of God. The disciples in Jerusalem experienced the power of God in a very tangible and real way. The place where they were gathered was shaken. When we pray, things will be shaken up. We will see the power of God at work in our lives and the world around us. So let's be obedient to the voice that comes through prayer and watch as God shakes things up!

The practice of prayer in a believer's life is an incredible, virtually untapped power source. Prayer moves the hand of God. Prayer prevails. Prayer turns ordinary mortals into men and women of power with the potential of God at their disposal. It is the key that unlocks the storehouse of God's riches. It is the call that moves heaven to act on behalf of the earth. Seek after God's potential that he has placed in us through prayer!

Chapter 8

Return: Where Do We Go from Here?

Nevertheless I have this against you, that you have left your first love. Remember therefore from where you have fallen; repent and do the first works, or else I will come to you quickly and remove your lampstand from its place—unless you repent.

—Rev 2:4–5

IF WE'RE NOT CAREFUL, we can jump ahead of God and think that we know how and when he is going to do a particular work in and through us. We can also get caught up in our own spiritual experiences and think that we have "arrived" only to find that we have not. The truth is that God is sovereign, and he will do things in His time and in His way. We need to be careful not to get ahead of Him or try to take matters into our own hands. Instead, we need to trust Him and be obedient to His leading. He will build His church and he will work in and through us according to His plan.

So let us be faithful to follow His plan and trust Him to work in us and through us for His glory. Hebrews 11:6 says, *Without faith it is impossible to please Him, for he who comes to God must believe that He is, and that He is a rewarder of those who diligently seek Him.*

God has a pattern for church revitalization, and we need to be the ones who are listening and being obedient to the voice that we hear. We need to be those who are being used by God to bring about change. We can't do it in our own strength, but with God all things are possible. Let us seek Him and trust Him to work in us and through us according to His sovereign plan.

In Acts 16:6–10 we see an instance in which Paul and his companions were trying to go into the province of Asia, but the Holy Spirit prevented them from doing so. Instead, they were directed by the Spirit to go into the region of Macedonia. This was not what they had planned or intended to do, but they were obedient to the leading of the Holy Spirit. As a result, they ended up planting the gospel in a strategic region that ended up having a great impact on the kingdom of God. We need to be careful that we don't get ahead of God or try to take matters into our own hands. Instead, we need to trust Him and be obedient to His leading. He will build His church and he will work through us according to His plan.

To be able to fully hear and be obedient requires our total and unconditional trust in the leading of God. Trust is a prerequisite to following without reservation. If we don't trust God, then we will always second-guess His leading and try taking matters into our own hands. But when we trust Him, we can be confident that he knows what he is doing and that he will work in us according to His will.

When we are totally surrendered and trusting in God, then we can be confident that God has this under control. We can know that no matter what the situation looks like, God is at work.

The question is not whether God is at work, but rather whether we are surrendered and trusting enough to follow His lead? Are we willing to be obedient to His leading even when it doesn't make sense to us? When we are surrendered to and trusting in God, then we can be confident that he is at work and will work through us according to His plan. And as we do, let us watch and see how he uses us to bring about His purposes.

Where do we go from here?

Moses knew that God's purpose for the Israelites was for them to be free from bondage in Egypt. But Moses had mistakenly thought he knew God's plan for how he would do it. Moses's story is a reminder that we need to know both God's purposes and His plan. We can know God's purpose for our lives by reading His Word and surrendering ourselves to Him. And we can come to know His plan by spending time with Him in prayer, asking for wisdom and guidance.

When we know both God's purposes and plan, we can live with confidence and hope, no matter what circumstances we find ourselves in. We know that God is at work, even when we don't see how things could work out.

In Exod 3:1–4:17 we see the story of how Moses was called by God to lead the children of Israel out of Egypt. But Moses wasn't sure he was the right man for the job. He didn't feel qualified, and he was afraid of what would happen if he failed. But God reassured Moses that he would be with him and that he would give him the strength he needed. So Moses agreed to do as God asked.

This is a great example of how we need to know both God's purposes and plan. We may not feel qualified for what God is asking us to do. But if we are surrendered to Him and trust that he will equip us for the task, then we can be confident that He will work through us to accomplish His purposes. God likes to demonstrate to the world and for ourselves that He can take the insignificant and do significant things with them.

Gideon is another example we can look at to see how God can work differently than we can see or imagine. Gideon thought he knew what God's plan was for defeating the Midianites. He thought it would take an army of 32,000 men. But God told Gideon that He would give him the victory with only 300 men. So he did as God asked and ended up winning a great victory.

This story shows us that we need to be careful not to assume we know what God's plan is. We need to be open to the fact that

God may have a different plan than we do and be willing to follow His lead even when it doesn't seem to make sense.

When we're willing to trust in God and rely on Him, we may be certain that He is at work and that He will use us to achieve His goals. There comes a moment of faith crisis that we must see God for who He is and the power that He holds in His hands alone. Let's try to trust God more fully so that we can be obedient to His direction. Let us therefore keep an open mind, and as we do so, let us observe how He works in us to accomplish His objectives. Let us be true to His design and trust God to work in us and through us for His good.

There are many wonderful small rural churches scattered throughout our country, and these dear people want to truly serve God and fulfill the obligation of the Great Commission. They know that they have a responsibility and have a desire to bless the communities they live in. But like Moses and Gideon, they assume that they know the plan that God has for their church ministry. Sometimes the intention is admirable, but the method is less than desirable.

Many times the leadership in these churches get together and try to figure out what they can do to increase attendance or make their churches more relevant. They look at the communities around them and see the need for food or clothing, and they decide to start food pantries or clothes closets. And while there is nothing wrong with helping those in need, these things are not always the best use of their time or resources.

These churches would be much better off if they spent more time praying and seeking God's guidance. They need to ask God what His plans are for their church, to seek His wisdom and direction so that they can be confident that they are doing what He wants them to do.

We need to be careful that we're not trying to force our plans and agendas onto God. We should be willing to surrender our ideas and plans to Him and trust that He knows what's best. When we do this, we can be confident that He will use us in ways we never could have imagined. Let us therefore pray that God would show us His plan and give us the wisdom and guidance to follow it without reservation.

In revitalization efforts many confuse action with effectiveness. They can mistakenly confuse doing something with accomplishing the best that God is intending for them. As the saying goes, "Don't let the good get in the way of the best." We may have good intentions, but if we're not careful, we can end up doing things that are not helpful or are even counterproductive.

What we need to do is take the time to seek God's guidance and wisdom. We need to ask Him what His plans are for us and then be obedient to His leading. When we do this, we can be confident that He will use us in ways that are far beyond our abilities.

Sometimes the intention is admirable, but the method is less than desirable. It is a good thing if your church wants to reach out into the community and serve in some capacity, but let the doing and good intention be directed by the Holy Spirit. You don't want to get in the way of what He is trying to do.

Pray that God will show you His plan and give you the wisdom and guidance to follow it. Ask for the courage to obediently carry it out even when it doesn't make sense to you. And trust that as you do, He will work through you to accomplish far more than you could ever ask or imagine (Eph 3:20).

With abundant enthusiasm, the church may say that Jesus commanded them to make Christlike disciples of all the nations, so they get to work. They embark on a mission trip to a needy area or country, start a Bible study for young adults, implement a Wednesday lunch for single mothers, and begin a Thursday night program for children. They might even conduct a children's camp. All of these are good things, of course, but they can too easily be done without any prayer or guidance from the Holy Spirit.

When we try to do things in our strength and for our glory, we will always fall short. We need to be humble enough to admit that we can't do anything without God. We need to rely on Him for strength and wisdom. The church was not commissioned to do *good* things but *God's* things. Our problem is that we don't think the way God does. God declared, *"My thoughts are not your thoughts, Nor are your ways My ways*" (Isa 55:8). When churches assume their thinking and planning are identical to God's, they try to accomplish God's work the world's way. It is naive thinking to assume God seeks to be glorified and make disciples of all the nations yet leaves the local church to figure out the details by themselves. We need to be careful that we are not just cogs in the wheel of the world's programs with a Christian label.

When we do things without guidance from the Holy Spirit, we will end up frustrated when our plans and methods will not work. We might as well not even bother because we will just be going through the motions. Any effort that is not of God can do some good things and might even spark some life in the ministry, but without God ordaining it, it will not fulfill the plan He has for that ministry. When we let God lead us, we can be confident that He will use us in ways that are far beyond our abilities.

Assuming you know God's plans?

God has a plan, and He is sovereign. He is in control. We must be careful not to try to take His place. When we do, we will only end up frustrated because our plans and methods will not work. We might as well not even bother, Jesus said, *"I will build My church"* (Matt 16:18). Christ not only builds His church but also directs His church. When Christ said He was the head of the church, He was not referring to a token figurehead. He was saying that He is in control. We must be careful not to try taking His place.

The revitalizing church must bear in mind that any activity that is not from God may be beneficial and may even produce life in the ministry, but it will not accomplish the purpose for which God has ordained it. Churches that are in the revitalization process can see some movement in the congregation, but without God's direction, it will be a limited success at best and short-lived.

A church that is truly being revitalized has been touched by God in a way that has given its people a new perspective. They have been changed. And when they go out and try to do the work of the ministry, they will quickly realize that they cannot do it in their own strength. They will need to rely on the Holy Spirit for guidance and strength. Only then will they be able to accomplish the task that God has set before them.

Revelation 1–3 shows that the risen Savior is active and involved with His churches. The churches are not just to exist as a moral example in society. The churches are to be active and do the work of the ministry that Christ has given them. The church is to be salt and light in the world (Matt 5:13–16). The church is to be a city on a hill that cannot be hidden (Matt 5:14). The church is to be a people set apart for God's use (1 Pet 2:9–10). The church is to be a people who proclaim the excellencies of Him who has called them *out of darkness into His marvelous light* (1 Pet 2:9).

The revitalized church will be one that's on fire for God. They will be people who are sold out to Christ and His cause. They will be people who are not afraid to speak the truth in love. They will be people who are not afraid to stand up for what is right, even if it means being persecuted for their beliefs. The revitalized church will be a people who are unashamed of the gospel of Christ.

We the church must be careful not to try to take the place of Christ. As Jesus Christ walks amongst His churches, He declares, *"I know your works"* (Rev 2:2, 9, 13; 3:1, 8, 15). To the church at Ephesus he says, *"You have left your first love"* (Rev 2:4). Christ is not only aware of what the churches are doing, but He also knows their hearts.

A church being revitalized has a new perspective and one that has been changed. Its people realize that they cannot do anything without God's help. They are humble and rely on the Holy Spirit for guidance. When we let God lead us, we may be certain that He will utilize us in ways far beyond our capacities. We must be wary of assuming His place. When we try to complete things on our own, we will almost certainly fail.

As the Lord dictated the letter to the Pergamos church, He found them living a little too close with idols (Rev 2:14–15). The church at Pergamos had people who held to the teaching of Balaam, which led the people of Israel into idolatry and sexual immorality. This church was also tolerating those who held to the teaching of the Nicolaitans (Rev 2:15). The Nicolaitans were a heretical sect who believed in antinomianism, which held that Christians are not bound by moral law.[1]

The Lord was very clear in His instructions to the church at Pergamos. He told them to repent and to turn away from their evil ways, warning them that if they did not repent, He would come against them with the sword of His mouth (Rev 2:16). The Lord is not someone to be taken lightly. He is a holy and just God who will not tolerate sin. We must be careful not to take His grace and mercy for granted.

The letter to the church at Pergamos is a wake-up call for the church today. We must be careful not to become complacent in our faith, to allow false teaching to creep into the church. We must be on guard against those who would seek to lead us astray and keep our eyes on Christ, not on the things of this world.

Many churches today walk around as if they are alive and healthy, but they are only dead men walking. The church at Sardis had a reputation for being alive but they were dead (Rev 3:1). This is a scary thought because it means that the churches today could be in the same condition. We could be going through the motions of being a church but could be missing the whole point.

The church at Sardis was told to wake up and *"strengthen the things which remain"* (Rev 3:2). This is good instruction for churches today. We need to wake up and realize that we are not doing everything we should be doing, that we have become complacent in our faith. We need to take a good, hard look at our churches and see if there's anything that needs to be changed, to make sure we're living according to the Word of God and not according to our own standards.

The church at Sardis was also told to hold fast to what they had (Rev 3:3). This is good instruction for churches, to hold firmly to the truth of the gospel, to the teachings of Christ, to the things we know are true. We need to be careful not to let go of the things we know are right.

1. "Antinomianism."

The church at Sardis was told to repent (Rev 3:3). We need to repent of our complacency, our apathy, and our indifference. We need to turn away from our sin and turn toward Christ.

The church at Sardis was told to be watchful (Rev 3:3). We need to be watchful for false teaching, for those who would seek to lead us astray. We need to be on our guard against the enemy, always to be alert and ready. They will not come to the church doors beating on them demanding that you start believing this false stuff, no, they slide in slowly and quietly.

The church at Sardis was told to be ready. (Rev 3:2). We need to be ready for Christ's return, to meet Him face to face. We need to be ready to stand before Him and give an account of our lives.

Probably the most famous of all the churches of Revelation was Laodicea. They had a temperature control problem. The Lord told them they were lukewarm and that He was about to spit them out of His mouth (Rev 3:16). This is a scary thought because it means that the churches today could well be in the same condition. We could be going through the motions of being churches, but we could be missing the whole point.

The church at Laodicea was told to be zealous and to repent (Rev 3:19). We need to be passionate about our faith, to be on fire for Christ, to be eager and willing to follow Him, to turn away from our sin and turn toward Christ.

The church at Laodicea was also told to buy gold from Christ (Rev 3:18). We need to seek after Christ, to desire Him more than anything else, to treasure Him above all else.

These are just a few of the things the Lord had to say to the churches in Revelation. But these are also good instruction for churches today. We need to take a good, hard look at our churches and see if there's anything that needs to be changed. We need to make sure we're living according to the Word of God and not according to our own standards, to be on our guard against false teaching, to be always alert and ready. And most of all, we need to seek after Christ with all our hearts. It was certain that none of these churches intended on displeasing the Lord. Their leaders probably believed in the efficiency of their methods. But God was not pleased. Sardis, Laodicea, and the other churches in Revelation all had something that needed to be changed. The same is true for churches today. We need to take a good, hard look at ourselves to see if there's anything that needs to be changed. We need to make sure that we are living according to the Word of God.

With God it is not just what you do that matters but how you do it and with what heart. Many churches across our land need a word from the risen Savior. Their programming is full, their calendars are running over, and their numbers may seem slightly ahead of last year. All may seem well, yet Christ would declare to them, "But I have this against you. I know your works!" (see Rev 2:2–3). We must not be deceived by mere activity. We need to be careful that our churches are not just going through the motions. We need to make sure that our hearts are in the right place.

We must not let our enthusiasm cloud our vision and understanding for how God wants to work in an area. The church was not commissioned to do good things but to do *God* things. When churches assume their thinking and planning is identical to God's, they try to accomplish God things the world's ways.

Is your church trusting God for your plans?

The key to honoring God is not to develop your own plans and then ask God to bless them. God already has a plan. The key is to cry out to God and to ask Him to reveal His plans to you. This is the process of God imparting His vision to you. As a church, you have the Holy Spirit present within you, who knows God's mind completely (see 1 Cor 2:9–12). His role is to guide you into the will of the Father.

The church must be a place where Christians may go to hear the gospel of Christ and understand God's plan for their lives. Christ not only builds His church, but He also directs His church. Christ is the captain of the ship. He determines the direction and destination. We need to be careful that we are following His lead and not our own. It's not just what we do that counts with God; it's also how we accomplish it and with what heart.

Chapters 1–3 of Revelation shows that Christ is active and involved with His churches but will also hold them accountable for how they conduct themselves. We must make sure that our churches are living according to the Word of God and not according to their own self-determined standards.

Prayerfully consider about whether your church needs a word from the risen Savior. Is there anything that needs to be changed? Are you living according to the Word of God or your own standards? Let us make sure that our hearts are in the right place as we follow Christ, the captain of our ship.

"To get anywhere you must take the first step of deciding you're no longer willing to stay where you are."

Chapter 9

Living in the Promise of Transformation

If My people who are called by My name will humble themselves, and pray and seek My face, and turn from their wicked ways, then I will hear from heaven, and will forgive their sin and heal their land. Now My eyes will be open and My ears attentive to prayer made in this place. For now I have chosen and sanctified this house, that My name may be there forever; and My eyes and My heart will be there perpetually. As for you, if you walk before Me as your father David walked, and do according to all that I have commanded you, and if you keep My statutes and My judgments, then I will establish the throne of your kingdom, as I covenanted with David your father, saying, "You shall not fail to have a man as ruler in Israel."

—2 Chr 7:14–18

The Lord is faithful to His promises, and if we will humble ourselves, pray, seek His face, and turn from our wicked ways, He will hear from heaven and forgive our sins and heal our land. This is His promise to us, and He is calling us to repent and return to Him with all of our hearts. He is waiting for us to come to Him, and He will never leave us or forsake us. He is our loving Father, and we can trust Him with all our hearts.

There is hope for our churches that are needing revitalization in a bad way. There is a set pattern that God ordained for us to start the process. That pattern is to turn to Him completely. When we do, He will work in us and then through us. We need to see our churches as God sees them and not how people see them. We also need to be careful not to get caught up in the cares of this world or the things of this world that can easily take our focus off of Christ. We need to keep our eyes fixed on Jesus, the author and finisher of our faith (Heb 12:2).

The world is desperately in need of the hope that only Christ can give, and we as His followers need to be His witnesses to a lost and dying world. We need to be living examples of His love, grace, and mercy. We need to be preaching the Gospel and sharing the hope that we have in Christ with everyone we come in contact with. We need to be living in the promise of God and trusting Him to do what He has promised. Are you living in the promise? Repent and return today!

God is a God of order and purpose. Amid difficult times, we need to remember this. We also need to keep our eyes on Jesus Christ—the One who was in the beginning, is today, and will be forever (Heb 13:8). When we do, we can be assured that He will never leave us or forsake us but will be with us always, *even to the end of the age*" (Matt 28:20). God wants to bring order back into your church and reignite your God-given purpose.

The most important part of God's gospel to us can be described in this one word: *transformation*. This is what we are called to—to be transformed from our sinful human nature and to partake of His glorious, perfect divine nature (2 Pet 1:4). And this transformation takes place as we allow the Holy Spirit to work in us and through us. It is not something that we can do in our own strength. We need to surrender our lives to Christ and let Him have His way in us.

Is your church living in the transformational power of God? We can go from absolute sinful wretches to perfect vessels of God's glory and goodness! No greater gift exists in all of creation. We need to allow the Lord to do this work in us so that we can be used by Him to reach a lost and dying world.

When we think of church revitalization, let's not limit God. He is able to do immeasurably more than all we ask or imagine (Eph 3:20). We need to have faith in God and trust that He is able to do what He has promised. Let's not get caught up in our limitations, but let's view things from God's perspective. He is able to do the impossible, and we need to step out in faith and trust Him.

Are we ready to see our churches transformed? If so, then let's surrender our lives to Christ and allow Him to work in us and through us. He is looking forward to our arrival, and He will never abandon or leave us. Come to Him now, and allow Him to turn your church around!

The term *renewal* refers to the many changes that a church undergoes over time and the process by which it is transformed. It implies renewing oneself with greater purpose and meaning. As an organization of faith, we understand ourselves as followers of Jesus Christ who are called upon to be witnesses in this world for those around us; it is incumbent upon us to continually seek ways in which we can better proclaim the good news and extend an invitation for others to join us on this journey.

At its core, renewal is about change—a reorientation of our lives and our mission as a church. It is a process that requires intentionality, prayer, and hard work. We hope that as you journey through the process of church revitalization, you will be encouraged and challenged to pursue transformation in your own life and the life of your church. We pray that God will reveal Himself to you in new and fresh ways and that you will be transformed by His power and presence.

When a church is in decline, it frequently has to reconnect with the essence of what God calls us to be. This often requires a time of soul-searching and self-examination. We must ask ourselves, "What does it mean to be the body of Christ in this particular place and time?" This is not an easy question to answer, but it is one that we must all wrestle with if we are to move forward in faith.

When we need revitalization within our churches, it's because we've lost touch with the people outside of our church's walls and those who aren't in our religious community; we devote all of our time, effort, and attention to members of our congregations but have stopped caring or even interacting with non-members. In doing so, we lose our mission and our way.

The church was never intended to be a self-contained entity; rather, it is called to be in the world but not of it (John 17:14–16). We are to engage with those around us, love them unconditionally, and share the good news of Jesus Christ with them. When we fail to do this, we not only prevent people from coming to know Christ, but we also miss out on the opportunity for our own lives to be transformed.

The process of church revitalization is often long and difficult, but it is worth it because it can lead to a deeper understanding of who we are as Christians and help us to better fulfill our mission in the world. It is our hope and prayer that you will join us on this journey.

The first step in the process of renewal is to seek God's face. We must humble ourselves before Him and ask for His wisdom and guidance. We need to repent of our sins and return to Him with all of our hearts (2 Chr 7:14). Only then can we begin to see things from His perspective and have clarity about the direction in which He is leading us.

The second step is to take an honest look at our current situation. This can be a difficult and painful process, but it is necessary if we are to identify the areas in which we need to grow and change. We must be willing to face the truth about ourselves, even when it's not pretty.

The third step is to develop a vision for the future. This requires us to imagine what could be and to dream about what God might do in and through us. It is important to remember that our vision must be grounded in Scripture and based on God's promises. We cannot allow our imaginations to run wild; rather, we must submit our plans to Him and trust that He will lead us forward.

The fourth step is to take action. This is where the rubber meets the road. We must put our faith into practice and begin living out our vision. This will require courage, perseverance, and discipline. We must be willing to step out in faith, even when we're afraid.

The final step is to continue in the process of renewal. This is a lifelong journey, not a one-time event. We must continually seek ways to grow and change. We must be willing to let go of the past and embrace the new things God is doing in our midst.

The process of church renewal can be difficult, but it is worth the effort. Pursuing transformation is an essential part of our calling as Christians, and it is something we must all be prepared to do. Let us journey together in faith, trusting that God will lead us forward into a bright future.

Some churches will embrace the revitalization and transformational challenge and have a renewed sense of purpose and power. Others will not. They will refuse to change or even acknowledge that there is a problem at all and will fade into memory. The difference between these two scenarios is a willingness to change. Without it, a church is just another building. With it, a church can be the hope of the world. So let us all be willing to change, to grow, to journey together in faith. It is our hope and prayer that you will join us on this journey. Depending on the level of a congregation's readiness to embrace change, one of these two options will be chosen.

It's simple to see if something isn't functioning; it's more difficult to figure out how to improve. Seeking God's wisdom is the first step. Take an honest look at your congregation's strengths and weaknesses to get a sense of where you are today. This can be difficult, but it will help set the stage for what's to come.

Developing a vision for the future requires imagination, creativity, and most importantly, prayer. Work together as a team to dream about what God might do in and through your church. Remember to keep your focus on Scripture and God's promises. Now it's time for action. This is where the real work begins. It will take courage, discipline, and perseverance to implement the changes needed to begin living out your vision. But it is so worth it! Remember that this is a journey, not a destination. There will always be room for growth and change. Embrace it! And invite others to join you on the path of renewal. Remember that the definition of insanity is doing the same thing over and over, hoping for a different result.

If your church isn't growing, if attendance is down, if you are having trouble reaching your community, it's time for a change. And that change starts with you. Will you be the one to take the first step?

Transformation is all about reconnecting us to our calling as a church in mission by changing who we are. *Metanoia* is Greek for "a change of mind" and refers to a person's effort to reconnect with God's will and aim. We must alter first as individuals, then as a congregation. The process of transformation can be difficult, but it's well worth the effort. Pursuing transformation is an essential part of our calling as Christians, and it's something we must all be prepared to do. Let us walk together in hope, confident that God will guide us toward a magnificent future.

Transformation involves listening to God, developing our relationship with God, and then acting on what we understand to be His will. We may frequently discover that improved health follows if we reestablish the spiritual link between God and the purpose of our institution. When we become more effective in our mission, we will also be healthier.

Seeking God's guidance is critical to transformation. You must be willing to hear what God is saying, even if it means making tough decisions. Be patient as you wait for God to reveal His plan. It may not happen overnight, but trust that He will lead you in the right direction. Transformation is a process, not an event. It takes time, patience, and perseverance. When we allow God to transform us, He can use us in ways we never thought possible. We become more effective witnesses for His kingdom and are better equipped to serve our communities.

This process is one where we need to admit that things need to change. This can be a difficult process, but it is so important. We must be willing to let go of our old ways and embrace new ways of doing things. This may mean changing the way we think, the way we worship, or even the way we do church. But if we are open to change, God can do amazing things in and through us. It's not our church; it's God's church.

We must take action. We must pray expecting God to answer. We must be willing to take faith risks together with God. We must act with confidence that God will bless our efforts.

The word *transformation* refers to a spiritual journey that has an intended beginning but no end; we are always on the road, never completed. Because it focuses on change in proactive intentional processes, transformation is a strategic trip. The goal of the church is to become a "best-in-class" ministry that both serves and empowers members, their friends, and the communities in which they live. The church has a clear vision for how to get there but may recast it as required.

The transformation that the church goes through must be a life-changing effect on the body and not just another program that they go through. It must change their worldview and change the attitudes of everyone for everyone. The overall goal of the church should be to be effective in its mission and to be healthy.

We become more effective when we reconnect with our purpose and live out our mission. When we are focused on God's will, we will be transformed into the people He created us to be. To become transformed, the church must be willing to let go of old traditions and ways of doing things. We must also be open to change and willing to embrace new ways of doing things. Additionally, we must seek God's guidance and direction in all we do. Finally, we must take action in order to implement the changes that are needed. When the church allows God to transform them, He can use them in ways they never thought possible. They become more effective witnesses for His kingdom and are better equipped to serve their communities.

A transformed church transforming their communities

A transformed church is full of the love of God. It's a church where people are passionate about their faith and are committed to living it out in their daily lives. When a church is transformed, its members become agents of transformation in their communities. They reach out to those who are lost and hurting, and they show them the love of Christ. They meet needs and help others to find hope. A transformed church is a powerful force for good in the world, and it all starts with each member being transformed by the power of God's love.

At the beginning of this book I talked about how God is a God of order and purpose. And the purpose of the church is to go into our community and tell others about Christ so they too can experience transformation. We become more effective when we reconnect with our purpose and live out our mission. When we are focused on God's will, we will be transformed into the people He created us to be. We need to be open to change and willing to let go of our old ways. This can be a laborious process, but it is well worth the effort! Allow God to transform you and watch as He does amazing things in and through you. Remember—transformation is a long-term endeavor, not a one-time event. It takes time, dedication, and fortitude to complete it.

As we allow God to transform us, we become more effective witnesses for His kingdom and better equipped to serve our community. We reach out to those who are lost and hurting and show them the love of Christ. We meet needs and help others find hope. Let us be transformed by the renewing of our minds, and let us go forth into our communities as agents of transformation, sharing the love of Christ with all we meet.

So what are you waiting for? Allow God to transform you today! Seek His guidance and direction in your life. Be open to change and willing to let go of old ways. Take action in your community. And watch as God does amazing things through you and your church. This is the power of transformation, and this is the pattern of revitalization that He has ordained as the way to spiritual and church health.

Bibliography

"Antinomianism." Theopedia, n.d. https://www.theopedia.com/antinomianism.

Bricker, Sophia. "Why Is God a God of Order?" Christianity, May 7, 2021. https://www.christianity.com/wiki/god/why-is-god-a-god-of-order.html.

Briefman, Elaine. "Invite Pastor Elaine." Fishing4Truth, n.d. https://fishing4truth.com/speaking/.

———. *Jesus Is In: Christian Counseling Simplified.* Browns Valley, CA: iM, n.d.

Tozer, A. W. *The Knowledge of the Holy.* New York: HarperCollins, 1961.

Vaters, Karl. "If Small Churches Are Essential, Why Are We Not Fulfilling Our Potential?" Karl Vaters, Jan. 24, 2022. https://karlvaters.com/small-churches-essential-potential/.

"What Does It Mean to Be God-Centered?" Got Questions, last updated Jan. 4, 2022. https://www.gotquestions.org/God-centered.html.